A CAREER GUIDE
for the HEALTH SERVICES MANAGER

3rd Edition

A CAREER GUIDE
for the HEALTH SERVICES MANAGER

3rd Edition

ANTHONY R. KOVNER
ALAN H. CHANNING

Health Administration Press
Chicago, Illinois

Cover photo credit: Images® copyright 1999 PhotoDisc, Inc.

04 03 02 01 00   5 4 3 2 1

Library of Congress Cataloging-in-Publication Data

Kovner, Anthony R.
    A career guide for the health services manager / by Anthony R. Kovner, Alan H. Channing. —3rd ed.
        p.   cm.
    Prev. eds. have title: Really trying.
    Includes bibliographical references and index.
    ISBN 1-56793-111-1 (soft : alk. paper)
    1. Health services administration—Vocational guidance.
    I. Channing, Alan H. II. Kovner, Anthony R. Really trying.
    III. Title.
    RA440.9.K68 1999
    362. 1'068—dc21   99-28565
                                                              CIP

The paper used in this publication meets the minimum requirements of American National Standards for Information Sciences—Permanence of Paper for Printed Library Materials, ANSI Z39.48–1984. ∞ ™

Health Administration Press
A division of the Foundation of the
    American College of Healthcare Executives
One North Franklin Street
Chicago, IL 60606
312/424-2800

For Chris, who was there with me
For Ronda, without whom I'd be lost

Contents

Foreword

WHAT I HAD HOPED TO ENCOUNTER IN *A Career Guide for the Health Services Manager* was as follows:

- where health services managers work (i.e., the types of organizations);
- how they get jobs in these institutions;
- what skills make a good manager and how these skills are obtained;
- the opportunities and challenges most managers face;
- how a manager "gears" into a management role;
- what a health services manager expects from, and what is expected by, the work force; and
- how a manager advances within an organization and within an industry.

I can assure the reader that all of my expectations were met—along with a few nice surprises. For instance, I did not expect this book to devote one exhaustive chapter to working with clinicians and the accompanying challenges that are faced by managers. Along with this chapter, I found extremely valuable the insights on managerial contribution to effective performance found in Chapter 3. I loved this chapter and found myself wishing that some of the managers I am lucky enough to work with would take a moment to reflect on it.

The authors' theme of worker empowerment is, from what my experience has taught me, something that unfortunately is not practiced often. Examples of "the effective and ineffective manager" add greatly to the value of this career guide. Chapter 4, "Finding Your Niche," is great for giving basic information on the direction one should take when deciding on a career. Chapter 5, "Managing Yourself," made very clear that trust is one of the most important "political capital" investments that managers can make. Another extremely important theme of this chapter is to "know your values and how they differ from your superiors'." The authors also give great advice about what the boss expects and how to relate to and work with the boss.

Overall, this career guide is an excellent book for aspiring health services managers. It is very well written and comprehensive, and it addresses the main factors in the industry, in the work force, and in obtaining a job.

Jacob O. Victory, MPA
Planning Associate
Cabrini Medical Center
New York, New York

Preface to the Third Edition

THIS IS A BOOK ABOUT MANAGERS IN HEALTHCARE FOR persons wanting this kind of a career. We have tried to tell it "like it is." Both of us have enjoyed rich working careers as health services managers, with all the ups and downs, and we have loved the work. We have been gratified by the response to the first two editions of our book, titled *Really Trying: A Career Guide for the Health Services Manager*, from students and practitioners. They have made, basically, two suggestions for the third edition. First, make the book a lot shorter; and, second, change the title. We have implemented these changes, but have tried in our update not to tinker with what was successful in the name of timeliness. What we've tried to keep in the book is a view from the field about what you need to know, how, and why, as experienced by the entering and mid-level health services manager. We would like to acknowledge the careful reading and helpful comments of Jacob O. Victory.

We encourage your comments and suggestions, as we would like to be in touch with our readers.

Anthony R. Kovner, Ph.D.
Professor, Robert F. Wagner
*   Graduate School of*
*   Public Service*
New York University
610 Tisch, 40 West 4th Street
New York, New York 10012
(212) 998-7444
ak6@is2.nyu.edu

Alan H. Channing
President & CEO
St. Vincent Charity Hospital
Saint Luke's Medical Center
2351 East 22nd Street
Cleveland, Ohio 44115
(216) 363-2797
ahc3@is8.nyu.edu

Acknowledgments

THE AUTHORS WOULD LIKE TO ACKNOWLEDGE the assistance of Yvonne Ellinor for providing research help in updating the statistics used in the text and reviewing early drafts from the prospective of a new graduate. We would also like to acknowledge the management staff at St. Vincent Charity Hospital and Saint Luke's Medical Center for sharing their use of electronic communications with us.

Health Services Organizations

The new model for healthcare: "a community-owned organization devoted to the delivery of comprehensive health care...that attempts to serve a large but defined population by competing for market share on the basis of both cost and quality, using strong economic and organizational ties with physicians and other health care professionals."

> — John Griffith, "Managing the Transition to Integrated
> Health Care Organizations," *Frontiers of Health Services
> Management,* 1996

We also identified those assets or efforts that could provide a substantial return on investment and those that could not. As a result, we exited some markets and divested substandard businesses.... These actions not only improved our bottom line; they freed up management's time and our associates' talent to concentrate on furthering our strategic successes.

> — David A. Jones and Gregory H. Wolf, *Humana Annual
> Report,* 1998

WHETHER THEY WILL EVOLVE INTO NATIONAL investor-owned corporations or local nonprofit community provider organizations, healthcare organizations can be viewed as having the following four performance requirements: they must achieve goals; they must maintain their operating systems; they must adapt to change; and they must

Table 1.1   Categories of Health Services Organizations

Type of Service Provided	Inpatient	Outpatient (Physician-Focused)	Community (Non–Physician-Focused)
Acute			
General	Hospital	Group practice Health maintenance organization Convenience clinic Neighborhood health center	Home health agency Day care center
Special	Maternity hospital Psychiatric hospital Eye, ear, nose, throat hospital Orthopedic hospital	Ambulatory surgery Mental health center	Ambulance service Clinical laboratory
Chronic			
General	Hospice	Day care center	Foster home
Special	Psychiatric hospital	Drug abuse clinic	Special housing

integrate the values of their workers with those of the organization. For a list of categories of health services organizations, including hospitals, group practices, and home health agencies, see Table 1.1.

GOAL ATTAINMENT

The goals of healthcare organizations are often similar to those of other organizations. Managers in hospitals, nursing homes, group practices, and health plans—like managers of hotels, restaurants, and auto companies—attempt to increase the number of customers and what they pay to purchase services from the organization. Such organizations may or may not have mission and vision statements and measurable goals and objectives, articulated in advance of a period of time, usually one year. For a sample mission statement, see Exhibit 1.1, and

Exhibit 1.1   Sample Mission Statement: Daughters of Charity Health
Ministry Mission, Vision, and Values

The Daughters of Charity health ministry advances and strengthens the healing mission of the Catholic Church through ideas, influence, and actions. We will be faithful to the tradition of service established by St. Vincent de Paul, St. Louise de Marillac, and St. Elizabeth Ann Seton.

Our *mission* is to make a positive difference in the lives and health status of individuals and communities. Central to our mission is service to those persons who are poor. The health services we provide will be spiritually centered, accessible, and affordable.

Our *vision* is a strong, vibrant Catholic health ministry in the United States in the 21st century. We are committed to partnering with those with whom we share compatible values, including other sponsors, physicians, and associates. We believe the laity are partners in sharing responsibility for the health ministry.

Our vision demands transformation and calls us to:

- Advocate for a humane and just society, with special concern for those persons who are poor and vulnerable.
- Emphasize a culture that embraces learning, diversity, collaboration, and the well-being of our associates.
- Strengthen the development of religious and lay leaders.
- Commit ourselves to all aspects of health—community health, personal health, disease management, and spirituality.
- Achieve a full continuum of care—a balance of home, community, ambulatory, and inpatient services—to meet preventive, acute, and chronic needs.
- Foster growth to strengthen the ministry through partnerships, acquisitions, and diversification.
- Invest in change by demonstrating the value of innovation.

We must transform our governance, service models, and thinking to continue our mission and achieve this vision. In keeping with St. Vincent de Paul, "Let us put confidence in our Lord, for He will be with us first and last in the accomplishment of a work to which He has called us."

Our core *values* inspire our mission and vision as the Charity of Christ urges us to: Respect, Quality Service, Simplicity, Advocacy for the Poor, and Inventiveness to Infinity.

Note: Reprinted with the permission of Daughters of Charity National Health System, St. Louis, MO.

for a sample vision statement, see Exhibit 1.2. For an excerpt of goals, objectives, and implementation strategies of a health services organization, see Exhibit 1.3.

With regard to goal attainment, healthcare organizations may differ from organizations in other sectors of the economy as having:

- greater difficulty identifying the nature and benefit of the services they provide;
- a less standardized production process; and
- less emphasis on profit and organizational growth.

SYSTEM MAINTENANCE

Healthcare organizations provide goods and services to patients or members in a variety of settings. Services provided include diagnosis, treatment, and continuing care. Core systems, or operations, provide support services essential to patient care such as transport, housekeeping, dietary, and communications. For an example of an organizational chart of a healthcare organization, see Exhibit 1.4.

Some of the distinctive characteristics of healthcare organizations in maintaining operations have included complicated and indirect reimbursement, expensive facilities and technology, labor-intensive services, and incentives favoring professional control.

ADAPTIVE CAPABILITY

In the face of rapidly changing medical technology and swings in governmental policy, many healthcare organizations have lacked effective adaptive mechanisms, in part because of their community service nature and loosely coupled medical work force. Organizations vary in the extent to which their managers provide the support services necessary to develop and adopt long-range plans. Plans commonly include information about the organization's mission, the nature of services provided to whom, and the organization's competitive position. Plans may include timetables for future initiation, expansion, dilution of services and programs, and how these are to be accomplished, as well as criteria for mergers and acquisitions, or being acquired or affiliating with other provider organizations. Because

Exhibit 1.2   Sample Vision Statement

Our Vision and Values
The Valley Hospital exists to serve the healthcare needs of our patients and their families. Our desire is to place the patient at the center of all that we do.

By doing what is best for the patient, we measure the success of all our activities and set a standard of care that cannot be surpassed.

It is our goal to reach for the highest standards of honesty and integrity in our medical and business practices, to nurture team accomplishments, and to develop the potential of each person.

Our values are those attributes of character which we regard as of highest importance in the pursuit of our vision.

Whatever our responsibility, we:
- Care about patients and each other
- Respect the dignity and value of all persons, their beliefs, feelings, and experiences
- Deal openly and honorably with those with whom we come in contact
- Take pride in the quality of our work
- Go one step further in pursuit of our mission.

These guiding principles enable our values to become reality. We seek to:
- Foster participatory management by empowering individuals throughout the organization to make decisions
- Maintain financial viability, cost effectiveness, and productivity
- Encourage staff creativity and innovation
- Promote open two-way communications and active listening
- Accept accountability as an individual and as a member of the team
- Provide and maintain up-to-date facilities and equipment
- Develop new programs based on existing hospital strengths and needs of the community
- Challenge individuals to further their personal and professional development
- Cultivate an environment that anticipates the future and responds with vigor to each challenge that comes our way
- Support a high level of involvement between the hospital and the community
- Work together as a dedicated team
- Treat others as they would want to be treated
- Recruit and retain high-caliber, dedicated, and committed people
- Recognize and reward achievement—celebrate success
- Provide compassionate, personalized caring services in response to our patients' physical, emotional, and spiritual needs.

Note: This document was conceived and created by the employees of The Valley Hospital and endorsed by the Board of Trustees, the Auxiliary, and the Medical Board. Reprinted with the permission of Valley Hospital, Ridgewood, NJ.

Exhibit 1.3   Excerpts from 1992–1994 Goals, Objectives, and
               Implementation Strategies of Greater Southeast Healthcare
               System, Washington, D.C.

Goal 1: Maintain or enhance the current operating margin of the Greater Southeast
         Community Hospital (GSCH).

Objectives:

A. Increase case volumes within Women's Health service line 10% over the 1991
   levels by the end of 1994.
   Strategies:
   1. Renovate and refurbish antiquated labor and delivery unit. (Completed
      November 1991.)
   2. Increase public and medical professional awareness of new facility and range
      of clinical and educational services available.
   3. Establish relationship with nearby public health clinic for referral of patients
      requesting hospital care at GSCH.
   4. Recruit at least two new OB/GYN physicians to establish private practices or
      join existing practices.
   5. Increase number of Medical Staff physicians taking emergency call for OB/
      GYN cases.

B. Enhance the current net revenue and profit levels of the Psychiatric service line by
   15% over 1991 levels by the end of 1994.
   Strategies:
   1. Convert 10 beds managed by contract group and previously dedicated to
      chemical dependency detoxification to Hospital control and treatment of
      psychiatric and drug-related diagnoses. (Completed 10/19/91)
   2. Develop outpatient aftercare rehabilitation programs for discharged chemical
      dependency patients.
   3. Maintain length-of-stay reduction efforts to reduce the average acute length of
      stay to 10 days by the end of 1994, from a length of 12 days in 1991....

Goal 9: Maintain or increase outside funding for community programs and initiatives.

Objectives:

A. Increase funding for community programs and initiatives by $2 million over 1991
   level ($140,000) between 1992 and the end of 1994.
   Strategies:
   1. Complete the Robert Wood Johnson Planning Grant process and submit
      proposal for funding for a 3-year hospital-led network of child health services
      in Ward 8.

Exhibit 1.3 Continued

2. Work with the Henry J. Kaiser Family Foundation to secure funding for a multi-year, community-focused Women's Health and Child Immunization program.
3. Develop relationships with The Commonwealth Fund and other philanthropic organizations and foundations and submit new program initiatives for funding.
4. Develop partnerships with local and federal government to secure funding for new program initiatives.

B. Increase funding in order to maintain existing community programs and initiatives by $2 million between 1992 and the end of 1994 over the 1991 level of $800,000.
Strategies:
1. Work with the local officials to secure Medicaid Eligibility status for the Ballou Adolescent Health Clinic.
2. Garner continued support and funding for current community-based programs including the *Breast Cancer Education Project*, the *Belva Brissett Women's Health Advocacy Center*, the *Neighborhood Blood Pressure Watch Program*, and the *Kellogg Foundation Community Connection*.

Source: Excerpted from the Greater Southeast Healthcare System Strategic Business Plan. Reprinted with permission of the Greater Southeast Healthcare System, Washington, D.C.

healthcare is largely produced locally, organizations vary in the extent to which those in charge have seen a need to adapt.

VALUES INTEGRATION

The values of health workers are shaped by their personal histories, situations, prior training, and experience. What people believe and prefer is affected by organizational characteristics such as history, size, complexity, and auspice. Some hospitals hire nurses and are selected by them as employers in large part because the hospital is owned by or affiliated with a particular religious group. What makes values integration difficult in health services organizations is a diverse work force and a fragmented authority structure.

ORGANIZATIONAL SETTINGS

In addition to the types of health services organizations shown in Table 1.1, a large number of organizations supply services to, or pay for, or regulate the services of healthcare organizations, such as:

Exhibit 1.4   Example of a Healthcare Organizational Chart

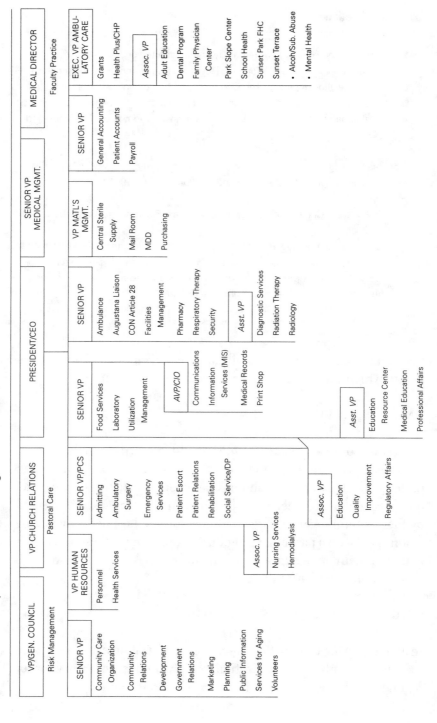

- management consulting and accounting firms;
- universities and research organizations;
- accrediting agencies and philanthropic organizations; and
- trade organizations, such as the local hospital or nursing home associations.

Organizations that pay for health services or who regulate health services organizations include the following:

- regulatory agencies at federal, state, and local levels;
- health plans, insurance carriers, and third-party payors;
- consumer groups and legislative offices; and
- large corporations, unions, and other purchasers of health services.

The list of healthcare settings—not to mention firms that sell to healthcare organizations—in which a manager can work is vast. Most of the managerial jobs are in insurance companies, pharmaceutical companies, HMOs and other managed care organizations, physician practice management companies, hospitals, group practices, nursing homes, home care agencies, governmental regulatory agencies, foundations, and trade associations.

Fourteen percent of our gross national product is in healthcare, and expenditures for payors translate into revenues for those who work in the sector. For example, as of 1999, there were more than 6,000 hospitals, 16,500 nursing homes, and 19,700 medical group practices. Although most of the dollars are spent in the hospital and physician sectors, 1995 pharmaceutical worldwide sales totaled $87 billion, with no major company holding more than an 8 percent share of the market.[1]

Most physicians work for themselves as private practitioners in medicine. However, between 1965 and 1991, the number of physician groups quadrupled from 4,289 to 16,576—an average growth of 475 groups per year. In 1996, the total physician membership in physician practice management companies exceeded 55,000 practitioners, or 8 percent of total physicians.[2]

More than 1,000 managed care companies operate in the United States. They differ widely in patient service, financial performance, and corporate culture. For example, Cigna HealthCare had 1996 revenues of $15.4 billion, covering more than 9 million people in 40 markets. As of March 1997, Cigna was the nation's largest managed care company. Cigna HealthCare is part of the Cigna Corporation, one of the largest U.S.-based international insurance organizations, with 1996 revenues of $19 billion and assets of $99 billion.[3]

Kaiser-Permanente is the nation's second largest managed care company, with 7.5 million members. Unlike Cigna, Kaiser-Permanente is a "mission-driven, not-for-profit enterprise," according to its annual report, that has "fiduciary responsibility to provide and demonstrate social benefit to the communities in which we operate." This enterprise is a partnership maintained among health plans and hospital organizations and medical groups, which are locally based contractors that provide care to health plan members.[4]

Many executives today may also work for non–acute care provider organizations. For example, Manor Care, which generates revenues of $1 billion annually, has 175 inpatient skilled nursing and rehabilitation facilities that provide three types of services: long-term care, high acuity services, and late-stage Alzheimer's care. Manor Care holds a controlling interest in Home Health, Inc, which provides healthcare services in 19 markets located in 13 states to clients in their homes. Services include skilled nursing, infusion therapy, hospice, rehabilitation, and personal care.[5]

We have drawn attention in the above examples to some of the larger sectors and companies because these are where one can find most healthcare jobs, including most of the managerial jobs. We discuss the range and types of managerial jobs in Chapter 2.

The environment that health services organizations face varies according to historical and competitive circumstances and the way in which their situation is perceived by key participants. Obviously, managers are better able to deal effectively with familiar situations; however, they may fail to perceive the differences between a new situation and previous ones, and, more often than not, they may attempt to use customary managerial methods that do not meet current circumstances. For example, the manager of a free-standing suburban community hospital that is the only hospital in town may respond adequately to external regulatory demands and adequately meet the needs of attending physicians in their private practices. But precisely because of this experience and how it has shaped the manager's perceptions, she may be ill-suited to manage a hospital of similar size and services that is part of a large hospital system and located in an inner city.

Thus, organizations and managers operating in 1999 may in a way be functioning as if they were operating in different time periods, relative to how other organizations function. Others may be functioning as if 1999 were the 1950s or as if 1999 were 2010. We would like to apply this type of "traveling in a time machine" perspective to managers working in five different health services organizations spanning a period of 50 years, from the late 1950s to the late 1990s. A summary of the performance requirements for these five organizations is shown in Table 1.2. (All represent ideal types based loosely on organizations in which one of the authors has worked or with which one of the authors has had extensive contact, either as a manager, a consultant, or a board member. An ideal type is a typical rather than an actual organization.)

The For-Profit Nursing Home (Late 1950s)

The goals of the small (60-bed) urban for-profit nursing home are to support the owner and to make a profit by providing nursing care, primarily to welfare patients. The nursing home must meet minimum standards of governmental licensing and paying agencies. It must have sufficient staff with adequate training to appropriately take care of patients and have sufficient working capital so that bills can be paid while awaiting government reimbursement. It must also have a manager who is able to deal with the complaints and suggestions of patients, relatives, and staff. Furthermore, this manager must be willing to market services to self-paying patients and their families.

Nursing home managers must respond effectively to changes in governmental regulatory standards and changing preferences or rules of agencies that refer patients and to which patients must be transferred. Necessary capital expenditures must be planned over time, or the nursing home must be sold before such capital expenditures are incurred.

The nursing home owner is the key values integrator; he attempts to meet the needs of patients within the constraints of the monies paid for their care. This must be done so that staff will continue to

Table 1.2   Performance Requirements for Certain Selected Organizations in Different Time Periods

Organization	Goals	System Maintenance	Adaptation	Values Integration
Nursing home (late 1950s)	Profit Owner needs	Referral and reimbursement	Compliance with regulations Recruitment and retention of nurses	High internal integration
Neighborhood health center (late 1960s)	Personal service and employment to local community Innovation to professionals	Government funding Hospital affiliation	Decreases in government funding Strivings of professionals Activism of community	Pluralistic groups with conflicting goals Low internal integration
University group practice (1970s)	Research Training	Practice income	Decreases in research Need for active recruitment of patients	High internal integration, not in tune with practice requirements
Rural hospital (1980s)	Avoid losses Recruit and retain medical staff	Capital funding Affiliations with other hospitals	Diversification of services	High internal integration
Community hospital/ healthcare system (1998)	Meet health needs of the community Survive financially	Government funding and rate setting	Affiliations for medical education Medicaid HMO	High integration between community and hospital goals

provide care of adequate quality, so that the residents' relatives will not be dissatisfied with the care to the point of attempting to transfer the patient or complaining to the authorities; and so that the owners will be able to make enough money to support themselves and their families and still have some free time for nonwork activities.

The Neighborhood Health Center (Late 1960s)

The primary goal of the large (215,000 physician visits per year) neighborhood health center is to meet the objectives and expectations of governmental funding agencies through the provision of personal service to and employment of neighborhood residents. A secondary goal is to support the professionals striving to provide innovative services in such circumstances.

Neighborhood health center management must ensure adequate governmental funding to meet licensing and regulatory standards, including building codes. Another system maintenance function is ensuring continued hospital affiliation and sufficiently acceptable pay and working conditions to minimize turnover of professionals.

Neighborhood health center managers must be adaptable enough to respond to reduced increases, or to decreases, in governmental funding. In the case of decreases, managers can consider marketing services to people who will pay for them, raising prices, collecting additional monies from people already receiving services, or scaling down operations to meet the funds available, without excessive staff turnover. Managers may also have to adapt constructively to pressures from community activities and government funders to drastically alter or end a hospital affiliation that has proven critical to recruitment and retention of innovative professional and managerial staff.

Responsibility for values integration is shared among managers and clinical, unit, and department heads. Regular meetings are held among managers with unit or departmental staff. Meetings are also held by managers with representatives of governmental funding agencies and the affiliated hospital to enhance perceptions of organizational compliance with governmental objectives. Meetings are held with community groups to generate support for continued funding, to enhance perceptions of the hospital affiliation, and to remain in compliance with government objectives.

The University Group Practice (1970s)

The goal of the recently formed group practice (fewer than ten FTE physicians at the outset) in a department of medicine is to obtain revenues to offset decreases in research grants—as long as this does not detract from the primary research and teaching goals of the department.

System maintenance requirements are modest; sufficient physician and support staff hours are needed to practice in existing facilities. Adaptive requirements are high because ways must be found to increase the number of patients who use the group's services. Such activities are difficult to undertake because private practitioners in the department resent such competition and because full-time physicians involved in teaching and research lack a competitive and practice orientation.

Integration of values is high within the group, but it is low between the group and part-time attending physicians in the same department. There is also some dissonance between the values of group physicians and the values of desired customers and their referring physicians. (For a more complete description of the group, see A. R. Kovner and D. Neuhauser, 1997, *Health Services Management: A Book of Cases, Fifth Edition*, Chicago: Health Administration Press.)

The Small Rural Hospital (1980s)

The goals of the small (50-bed) rural hospital include avoiding financial loss and recruiting and retaining a medical staff of adequate quality. The rural hospital must have sufficient admissions of patients who do not stay too long in the hospital, because one Medicare outlier under diagnosis-related groups (DRGs) can have a significant financial impact on hospital operations. Facilities must be adequate for attracting and retaining medical staff and adequate technical support staff.

Hospital managers can adapt effectively by reaching mutual accommodation with neighboring and urban hospitals to partition clinical services and share support services. Rural hospitals may have to diversify into chronic and ambulatory care to survive, as inpatient occupancies have fallen.

Small rural hospitals often have a high integration of values, not only among managers, trustees, and medical staff, but also among patients and health workers. Problems in integration can occur when working cooperatively with other hospitals, when diversifying into long-term care, or when key individuals have serious conflicts over resources.

The Large Community Hospital/Healthcare System (1998)

The large community hospital has recently reorganized into a health system. Now under one board of trustees is a large nursing home, a large neighborhood health center, an HMO with 30,000 members, and several other corporations (see Exhibit 1.3.) The healthcare system is located in a large city and has prided itself in serving the neighborhoods in which it is located. For one large low-income neighborhood, this has included providing services as disparate as housing for the elderly, language training for immigrants, and an HMO for Medicaid beneficiaries. Current goals as of 1998 include the following: to increase market share; to position itself as an essential managed care contracting partner; to develop an expanded, market-responsive, and integrated complement of physicians to position for success through strategic partnerships; and to maximize integration of parts within the health system.

System maintenance requirements include recruitment and retention of doctors and nurses to a low-income neighborhood, affiliations to continue medical education programs, and capital financing to maintain and reconfigure the existing plant.

Adaptive requirements include responding to state deregulation and reductions in funding and to mergers and aggressive, competitive initiatives by neighboring hospitals, many of whom have combined to form larger healthcare systems. The healthcare system currently has loose affiliations with a large metropolitan regional medical center–based health system and with the local medical school for residency programs. The healthcare system is considering combining, on several alternative bases, with a larger healthcare system adjacent to it, under a governance that is 50 percent from each system.

Integration of values has been high because of the constant dissemination of the hospital's (now the health system's) mission, which has resulted in external recognition of the hospital's excellence in serving its communities, and because of the long tenure of top management. A great deal of cultural diversity exists in the population served, reflected to an extent in the demographic characteristics of hospital employees. Integration of healthcare system values is seen as being threatened if there is a merger with the adjacent healthcare system, which is sponsored by a different religious group, and for physicians, particularly specialists who see themselves as threatened by future system-integrating initiatives that may have an impact on their practice and autonomy.

SUMMARY

This chapter has presented a framework for viewing healthcare organizations, including performance requirements of goal attainment, system maintenance, adaptation, and integration of values. We have briefly reviewed various types of organizational settings and provided snapshots of healthcare organizations as functioning during different decades.

We are trying to convey to the reader something of the vast size and changing dynamics of the health sector—roughly 14 percent of the nation's gross national product—whose employers range from the large healthcare system or investor-owned national corporation to the many small group practices, nursing homes, or home health agencies. Managers work in all of these settings.

As of 1999, many health services organizations are growing rapidly through affiliations and mergers. For example, many community hospitals are merging into vertically integrated healthcare systems, which may include several hospitals, nursing homes, and group practices. Physicians are increasingly working with other physicians in group practices and in larger group practices that have affiliations with a variety of HMOs or with one health plan. Moreover, some physicians work in groups that own their own HMO or health plan, one that may be owned, in turn, by an investor-owned and publicly traded physician practice management corporation.

Health Services Managers

"His manner often brash, reflecting the bravado required to build so
ambitiously, to attempt the different experiments, he is deeply cau-
tious, aware of the lurking dangers of bankruptcy, of incompetence,
of hubris, painfully aware that the power to persuade carries with it
the responsibility not to mislead."

— Dorothy Levenson, "Martin Cherkasky at Montefiore,"
Montefiore Medicine, 1981

THERE ARE MANY WAYS TO EXAMINE THE JOBS that health services managers do. In this chapter, we deal with managerial job descriptions, roles, activities, skills and experience, and education.

Figure 2.1 shows the relationships among role sets, activities, skills,
and functions of the manager. For example, the top function listed,
managerial planning, involves the role sets of motivating others, scanning, negotiating political terrain, and generating and allocating resources. The activities associated with the planning function include
recruiting staff, devising work procedures, and so on. Planning requires communications and analytical skills and experience, and individually, planners, like other managers, have certain demographic
characteristics, beliefs, styles, personalities, and educational backgrounds.

JOB DESCRIPTION

A job description is a way of looking at what the manager does or, by
implication, does not do. The position description of a hospital chief
executive officer is shown in Exhibit 2.1; that for a senior project leader
in a group practice HMO is shown in Exhibit 2.2.

Figure 2.1   Managerial Functions, Role Sets, Activities, Skills, and Persona

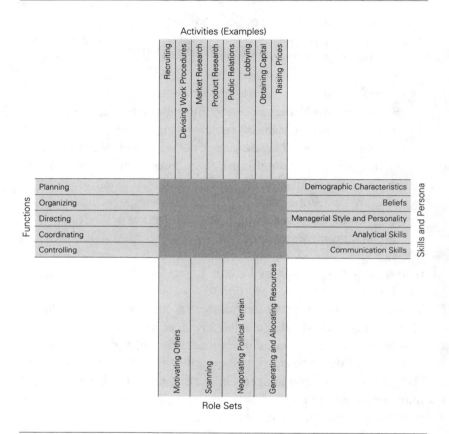

Implicit in these job descriptions are managerial functions, each of which comprises a group of managerial activities. Longest[6] views basic managerial functions as the following:

- Planning—the determination of objectives.
- Organizing—the structuring of people and processes to accomplish the work required to meet the objectives.
- Directing—the stimulation of members of the organization to meet the objectives.
- Coordinating—the conscious effort of assembling and synchronizing diverse activities and participants so that they work toward the attainment of objectives.

Figure 2.2   Managerial Roles, Functions, and Organizational Performance
Requirements

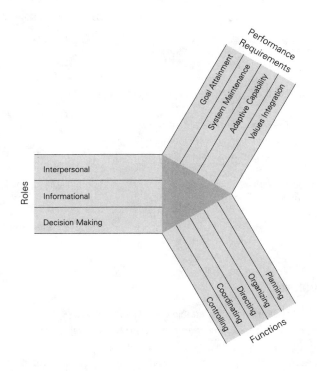

- Controlling—the comparison of actual results with
objectives to provide a measure of success or failure.

MANAGERIAL ROLE

Another way of conceptualizing what health services managers do is to
analyze their roles. Roles are aspects of behavior that can be abstracted
for analytical purposes. Managers have to settle conflicts, lead others,
and represent the organization to outside groups. These roles can be
viewed as part of the manager's functional responsibilities or they can
be viewed as aspects of the managerial contribution to organizational
goal attainment or system maintenance. A pictorial view of the interre-
lationship of roles, Longest's functions, and the organizational performance requirements specified in Chapter 1 is shown in Figure 2.2.

Exhibit 2.1   Position Specification: Chief Executive Officer, Community
Medical Center

RELATIONSHIPS

Reports to:
Community Medical Center Board of Trustees

Manages:
Management team of the Community Medical Center, which
currently includes:
- Executive Vice President, Finance and Information Systems
- Executive Vice President and Chief Operating Officer
- Executive Vice President, Ambulatory Care

Key Working Relationships:
- Community leaders
- Church leaders
- Medical staff
- Directors
- Regulators

MAJOR RESPONSIBILITIES

- Designing and implementing a strategic vision/plan for CMC.
- Effecting appropriate management and clinical program development and integration.
- Providing leadership and guiding the medical staff through current market conditions reflecting the competitive and rapidly changing marketplace. This leadership will require the development and implementation of new relationships between doctors and the medical center.
- Keeping the board and its leadership fully up-to-date and informed regarding the dynamic changes taking place in the healthcare marketplace.
- Assisting the board in developing appropriate and sensitive governance structures that reflect and respond to the needs in the community.
- Playing a highly visible leadership role in the community as the primary representative and spokesperson for CMC.
- Developing a strong and collegial management team.

KEY SELECTION CRITERIA

- Background exposure or understanding of the issues and dynamics surrounding the changing healthcare environment today. Particular experience in managed care, work redesign, and system integration.

Exhibit 2.1 Continued

- An established, effective track record in responding to a rapidly changing managed care marketplace.
- Unquestioned physician relation skills and experience with an exposure to a variety of physician/hospital organizations.
- Experience in developing primary care outreach services that are compatible with an overall system providing a wide variety of medical and healthcare services.
- Values consistent with CMC's service mission, including its charity care role.
- A visionary leader with strong communication skills. A track record and significant fund raising may be a plus.
- The personality, style, and interest to relate effectively to the board of trustees, medical staff, communities, and hospital employees.
- Experience working in or leading an important healthcare organization.

IDEAL PROFESSIONAL AND PERSONAL PROFILE

The successful individual for this position will have the following executive experience and talent:
- Experience in managing a complex healthcare organization through significant internal and external change.
- Experience in tough markets with consolidations, mergers, acquisitions, and downsizing.
- A strong record of accomplishment in building a highly successful healthcare enterprise.
- Well-established and effective relation skills with direct experience and exposure to a variety of new configurations and approaches that involve physician-hospital organizations and entities.
- Strong negotiation skills and experiences with a business orientation and a results-oriented approach to delivery of high-quality care.
- An individual with CEO experience or chief operating experience in a complex organization who can combine local leadership with effective communication in interrelationships.
- An executive who is open, trusting, and team-oriented, taking full advantage of the multiple talents within the organization and various constituencies that make up CMC.
- A community leader with strong personal presence and command.
- An ambitious but community service–oriented individual with high energy and the ability to inspire confidence within and throughout the organization.
- A person who shares the values and mission of CMC.

Exhibit 2.2   Position Specification: Senior Project Leader, Group
               Practice HMO

DEPARTMENT

Reports to: Director, Service Improvement Group

PURPOSE

The primary function of the senior project leader is to supervise, organize, and facilitate service improvement projects throughout the HMO in support of our strategic plan. This includes designing projects, developing practical solutions, and implementing and institutionalizing change and supervising HMO and medical group personnel on service improvement projects.

SPECIFIC DUTIES AND RESPONSIBILITIES

*   Supervise personnel and organize and facilitate the natural work team process in developing straw models, pilots, and/or implementations of solutions for service improvement opportunities.
*   Design and develop a continuous improvement plan for each service improvement project to follow up on implemented improvements and facilitate integration of results throughout the HMO system. Utilize resources within and outside HMO, useful to project implementation.
*   Conduct independent analysis of existing processes, identify root causes of opportunities to improve service, and develop project approaches in cooperation with the project executive client of the plan, group, or affiliate. Design, develop, and produce reports and documentation of results to the executive client and senior management of HMO.
*   Plan, support, and cooperate with SIG members to work as a team for managing change. Consult with other senior project leaders to provide feedback and insight in determining alternative solutions to problems. Train project leaders in service improvement skills.
*   Actively encourage participation of physicians and other HMO managers to implement project goals. Train and coach clients in change management tools to enable local managers to have a resident resource/skill base.

DECISION MAKING

*   Exercises discretion in determining project scope, approach, and time to completion. Has direct responsibility and accountability for meeting project deadline and deliverables. Exercises proper judgment in handling confidential information and data concerning the operation of HMO, medical groups, and affiliates.
*   Discretion and political awareness is crucial in dealing with medical groups. Improper use of judgment may result in damaging the reputation of HMO with the executive client and wasting of resources and time.

Exhibit 2.2 Continued

SUPERVISION

The incumbent supervises HMO and medical group personnel assigned to SIG projects and will additionally supervise future project leader hires.

CONTACTS

The incumbent has regular and frequent contact with the medical groups' senior management, group medical directors and regional administrators, hospitals and affiliates, and all other HMO departments. The senior project leader deals with the group medical directors and senior management on important and sensitive topics, provides counsel to them on issues facing the medical groups and the plan, and seeks support from various departments for their expertise.

KNOWLEDGE, SKILLS, AND ABILITIES

- Ability to supervise personnel assigned to his or her project, including establishing priorities, resolving personnel conflicts, and contributing to the performance appraisal of the assigned staff.
- Meeting facilitation and presentation skills, and the ability to coordinate problem solving and team building.
- Excellent interpersonal skills and political correctness awareness when dealing with other HMO systems. Excellent oral and written communication skills sufficient to interact with all levels of staff and senior management. Ability to build effective client relationships and enthusiasm.
- Ability to gather and analyze data to determine causes of service problems and design projects to address these opportunities.
- PC skills sufficient to produce documentation and reports for distribution to senior management; knowledge of Macintosh and its various software and graphic packages.
- Must be able to perform job duties as an independent professional and as a team player; organization skills sufficient to set own priorities, plan project scope, and facilitate work team progress.
- Must have a valid driver's license.

EDUCATION AND EXPERIENCE

A bachelor's degree in business, finance, HR, health analysis or policy, or any other related field. Advanced degree preferred. 5+ years' experience in an insurance, healthcare, or service environment is preferred along with PC skills. 6–8 years' experience in a business function within a healthcare environment may be substituted for the degree. Project leadership skills and change management experience are required.

Figure 2.3   Mintzberg's Managerial Roles

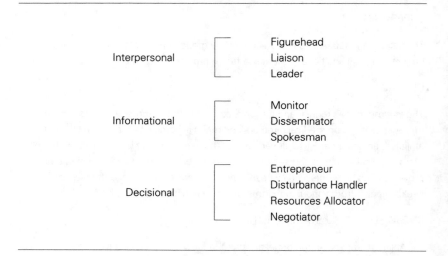

Interpersonal	Figurehead Liaison Leader
Informational	Monitor Disseminator Spokesman
Decisional	Entrepreneur Disturbance Handler Resources Allocator Negotiator

The roles of a manager can be abstracted from the rest of his or her personal behavior, which can help in understanding the managerial contribution to organizational performance and the constraints on and opportunities for such contribution.

Mintzberg's Managerial Roles

Henry Mintzberg has specified ten managerial roles, as shown in Figure 2.3.[7] He derived these roles from observing the work of five chief executives in a variety of organizations from 1967 through 1968. (One of the CEOs was the administrator of a large urban hospital.) Mintzberg divides the ten roles into three role categories: interpersonal, informational, and decisional. In other words, managers work with others, process information, and make decisions.

Mintzberg argues that production managers, sales managers, and staff specialists tend to concentrate their time in different managerial roles. Production managers (e.g., a hospital department head) place emphasis on the decisional roles, particularly those of disturbance handler and negotiator. For the sales manager (e.g., the director of marketing for an HMO), the interpersonal roles of figurehead, liaison, and leader appear to be the most important. The most important role of

Figure 2.4   Mintzberg's Roles Reconceptualized into Role Sets

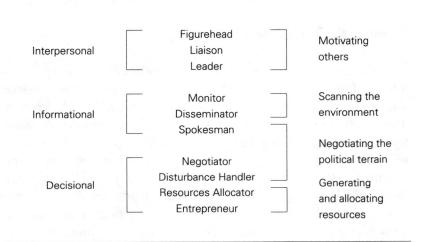

the staff specialist (e.g., the financial officer of a neighborhood health center) is that of a monitor and spokesman.

There is nothing sacred about Mintzberg's ten roles. In fact, Quinn's reconceptualization of Mintzberg specifies eight managerial roles: mentor, innovator, broker, producer, director, coordinator, monitor, and facilitator.[8] We have reconceptualized Mintzberg's ten roles into four role sets: motivating others, scanning the environment, negotiating the political terrain, and generating and allocating resources (see Figure 2.4).

Motivating Others

Managers spend a great deal of their time recruiting and retaining managerial and supervisory staff and in making decisions about rewards and promotions, work procedures, and development and training. To carry out these activities, managers use communications and analytical skills. Managers assist their subordinates in doing what is required as well as in doing what subordinates want to do, within organizational limits, which can be difficult, especially if managers have not recruited their subordinates. Even when managers have recruited subordinates (and recruitment is more of an art than a science), the recruitment and retention past one year of a high-performing subordinate is closer to 60 percent than 85 percent probability.

Scanning the Environment

Effective managers scan or search the environment for potential problems and targets of opportunity. Scanning activities include market and product research, long-range planning, and quality improvement. The development of management information systems may be essential for effective scanning. In large health services organizations, scanning activities are usually performed by special units like marketing, quality assessment, development, and planning. In smaller organizations, managers may scan the environment themselves or with the assistance of subordinates or colleagues. Information about what similar organizations and managers do is available from journals, books, newsletters, advertisements, and the Internet. Managers attend continuing education and trade association meetings where colleagues and experts discuss organizational and managerial opportunities and problems. Managers visit similar (and different) organizations to learn firsthand about possible ways to improve effectiveness and efficiency. Openness to such visits has been a characteristic of public and non-profit health services organizations.

Negotiating the Political Terrain

Effective managers maintain trust and build alliances with groups and individuals. A positive political climate contributes to effective decision making and implementation. New managers must find out "who is doing what to whom" in their organization; or, put another way, "what is the ballpark in which I am playing, who are the players, and what are the rules?" Managers learn the informal organizational power structure by reading and listening. The operative rules are not always easy to ascertain; they vary by organizational setting and they depend on the issue being discussed. Stakeholders establishing a joint laundry are different from those who decide to establish a renal dialysis unit.

Negotiating activities include public relations, lobbying, labor relations, persuading governing boards and medical staffs, arbitrating among internal units and departments, and making alliances with other organizations.

Generating and Allocating Resources

Effective managers spend a great deal of time analyzing organizational efficiency and finding ways to increase revenues and decrease expenses while considering past performance in their organization, performance of similar organizations, and industry standards.

They attempt to improve financial performance in buying procedures, securing long-term and working capital, building and maintaining equipment, and analyzing price changes and new construction. They specify how special circumstances influence preferences among alternative objectives and strategies, and they listen closely to arguments and rationales of subordinates and clinicians before making decisions.

Effective managers continually have to make decisions about generating and using resources as part of the budgetary process and in response to emergency or extraordinary requests. Less tangible resources, such as staff time, must also be allocated, as must resources less amenable to negotiation, such as space.

ACTIVITIES

Robert Allison, William Dowling, and Fred Munson developed a list of 46 organizational activities that are performed by managers of hospitals, nursing homes, group practices, and HMOs.[9] In their survey of six chief executives in each of these four types of organizations (24 in all), 32 of the 46 activities were determined to be crucial by one or more of the four types of executives. Twenty-five years later the list would probably be quite different; for example, it would probably include advocating for patients and consumers or even promoting community health.

Because many organizations have undergone significant restructuring, managers may carry the weight of several roles simultaneously. A laboratory manager can be responsible for the production of laboratory results, the marketing of services to attending physicians, the respiratory therapy service, and improving clinical documentation.

Managerial scope is broadening as the number of managerial layers is being reduced.

Exhibit 2.3 groups Allison et al.'s 32 activities into the four role sets discussed earlier (see Figure 2.4): motivating others, scanning the environment, negotiating the political terrain, and generating and allocating resources.

SKILLS

The manager works by using communications and analytical skills. Communications skills include reading, writing, speaking, and listening. Analytical skills include judging and deciding carefully.

Communications Skills

Managers spend more time communicating than deciding, but communications skills are usually underemphasized relative to analytic skills. Norman Urmy indicated in an interview (we can substitute "computer" for "calculator") that:

> Hospital administration is not about sitting in your office with a calculator.... About ten percent of the job is pushing paper, bureaucratic work.... Although I may have gone to six meetings and put in a ten-hour day, sometimes I feel I didn't get anything done.... The primary function of a hospital administrator is to provide integration and coordination within the hospital.... This means meetings and talking with people.[10]

Although communicating and deciding can take place simultaneously, lengthy communication often takes place before decision making and is crucial to successful implementation.

Managers receive numerous e-mails, voice-mail messages, and written materials and must generate similar output. Managers typically suffer from overload and lack adequate time to reflect on their work unless they manage their schedules accordingly. Reading, of course, includes analyzing numbers as well as concepts or service plans. Being

Exhibit 2.3   32 Crucial Managerial Activities, Grouped by Role Set

Motivating Others
- Recruiting professionals and physicians
- Decisions regarding professional and managerial salaries
- Devising work procedures for professionals
- Devising work procedures for nonprofessionals
- Promoting and rewarding professionals and managers
- Employee and management development and training
- Disciplining professional and managerial employees
- Motivating and directing immediate subordinates
- Dealing with personal and interpersonal problems

Scanning the Environment
- Market research
- Produce research
- Long-range planning
- Developing criteria systems to control quality
- Decisions regarding financial and management information systems

Negotiating the Political Terrain
- Public relations
- Lobbying
- Labor relations
- Establishing agreements with other organizations
- Negotiating with powerful external organizations
- Creating and changing professional job unity
- Decisions regarding changes in decision making and authority structure
- Influencing decisions of board or owners
- Influencing decisions made by medical staff
- Arbitrating between internal units and departments
- Arbitrating between policymaking groups

Generating and Allocating Resources
- Determine buying procedures
- Obtain long-term capital
- Obtain working capital: collections
- Decisions regarding maintaining building and equipment
- Decisions regarding charges and prices for services
- Decisions regarding new construction
- Decisions regarding housekeeping

Source: Adapted from R. F. Allison, W. L. Dowling, and F. C. Munson. 1975. "The Role of the Health Services Administrator and Implications for Education." In *Education for Health Administration,* vol. 2. Chicago: Health Administration Press, 147–84.

able to interpret numbers critically is an important skill that must be learned. Communicating a meaning for the numbers that can lead to an action recommendation is a skill that helps make a manager more successful.

By the time a future manager has reached graduate school, he is expected to have excellent reading and writing skills. If this is a weak area in your skill repertoire, we strongly encourage you to arrange for remedial assistance.

Listening and speaking effectively are as important as skill in reading and writing. Although managers know that public speaking can be learned, many are not aware that reading, writing, and listening skills can be learned as well. Managers can learn to make focused yet personal phone calls. They can learn to conduct meetings that accommodate goals and at the same time make attendees feel that their points of view have been listened to and their feelings have been adequately taken into account.

With the increasing diversity of the work force, the appropriate use and understanding of language becomes even more critical. Managers must ensure that organizational communications are understood by all. Use of carefully chosen language and symbols that are culturally sensitive can assist in messages being heard throughout the organization. For example, the culturally sensitive manager will be aware that many Latinos will take offense at finger pointing and refrain from that gesture. Similarly, staff who have learned English as a second language must be careful not to use words inappropriately or speak in a manner that unintentionally gives offense.

Listening and giving the sincere appearance of listening are important. So is hearing what people are not saying as well as what they are saying, as most people carefully choose what they say. Among the reasons for poor listening are: a lack of practice; preoccupation with one's own ideas and opinions; preoccupation with other matters; thinking much faster than others are able to talk; and lack of common ground for understanding (people fully understand only 25 percent of what they hear). There are several approaches to improving listening and hearing skills, including recapitulating a speaker's main points, numbering these points in importance, maintaining eye contact to avoid distraction, showing interest (asking oneself how to show genuine interest), and reacting with related questions.

In addition, it is now obvious that today's manager must be competent at the computer. It doesn't hurt as well to know how to operate voice mail and the fax and copy machines. The manager must know how to make use of electronic communications, for e-mail and for long-distance learning.

Analytical Skills

Of clear managerial importance are the analytical skills of judging and deciding. Ray Brown has defined "judgment" as knowledge ripened by experience.[11] Many feel that skill in judging and deciding can only come from experience, that it cannot be learned in school. Others argue that by analyzing and responding to managerial situations as structured cases or simulation, with participants taking parts or playing roles of different actors, judgment and decision-making skills can be improved. And experience can be meaningfully organized at work to ripen knowledge under close supervision by managerial coaching.

Before managers can effectively judge or decide, they must be able to define or frame a problem or situation, gather data, structure alternatives, and calculate benefits and costs for each alternative. Each step of this rational problem-solving approach involves judging and deciding. For example, how valid and comparable is the manager's definition of the problem relative to that of key clinical chiefs? What specific data should be gathered and what portion of the manager's time should be allotted to this task?

Computation skills are also required, for example, in making decisions on appropriate scheduling of patients for appointments, discounting the value of money over time to assess the true cost of capital financing, or pricing services to different payors so that revenues can be maximized. Computation skills include familiarity with frequently used computer software packages, such as those used in manipulating spreadsheets for alternative budgets or forecasting impacts.

COMPETENCIES

Daniel Goleman has grouped managerial capabilities into three categories: purely technical skills like finance and business planning; cognitive abilities like analytical reasoning; and competencies showing emotional intelligence such as the ability to work with others and effectiveness in leading change. Goleman found that emotional intelligence proved to be twice as important as the others for managerial performance at all levels.

He has categorized the five components of emotional intelligence at work as follows: self-awareness, self-regulation, motivation, empathy, and social skills.[12] The manager with a high emotional intelligence is self-confident, trustworthy, optimistic, cross-culturally sensitive, and has expertise in building and leading teams, among other characteristics.

PERSONA

The effectiveness of managers is determined as much by who they are and how they do things as by what they do. Managerial persona includes demographic characteristics, beliefs, style, and personality.

Demographic Characteristics

Many managers believe that how they manage, rather than what ethnic or other group they belong to, is what affects how others view their contribution. However, many people, including managers, feel more comfortable with and are more trusting of those whom they see as similar to themselves.

Stakeholders sometimes react to managers primarily in terms of "Is she one of us?" or "Is she part of some other group whom we dislike or fear?" The group practice administrator in a coal-mining community in western Pennsylvania may have great difficulty gaining the trust of a union-dominated governing board of Italians and Poles when she is herself well-educated, Syrian, and from a wealthy suburb of Philadelphia. This is a common problem, as well, for persons of minority sexual orientations such as gays, lesbians, and transsexuals.

Holidays are an example of how organizational demographics can play a cultural role. Management must be sensitive as to which holidays to represent to provide a diverse staff with appropriate time off and to avoid offending anyone.

Beliefs

People trust each other partly because of what they think are others' beliefs. "If she believes the same things I do, perhaps it doesn't matter so much whether I like her. I feel I can trust her because she is likely to do what I think she should do in a particular situation."

Professional nurses may distrust managers who they believe are interested only in money and who they think have little or no commitment to providing high-quality patient care. They may see managers in general as holding such beliefs. Such distrust can usually be overcome only over time, as managers' beliefs become evident by what they say and how they behave.

Style

Managerial style is subjective, elusive, and difficult to generalize about. Some managers adopt different styles depending on whom they are talking to. Style can be defined as the way managers perform their functions or roles and what they disclose about themselves in communicating with others. Style can be learned by observing how managers behave in different situations. Although management style may be easily differentiated and distinctly perceived by others, the manager may be the last to know he is seen as behaving differently.

Personal appearance is one aspect of style. In most organizations, clinicians distrust or show little respect for a manager with a shaggy mustache, uncombed, long hair, no tie, and loose-fitting clothes. On the other hand, in a free clinic, such a managerial style may make sense, may even make performance more effective.

Formality in speech and behavior is another aspect of style. Does the manager address others initially by their first names? Does the manager initiate or encourage conversations on personal matters, such as marital problems? Does the manager stand when someone enters the office? Does the manager encourage an open-door policy for all staff? Does the manager routinely take phone calls when meeting with a clinician? Is the manager's desk cluttered, very cluttered, or bare? Is the manager's office richly furnished or simple and plain?

Style can be learned and it can help or hinder managers being trusted by others. Some of the style changes adopted at work by the authors include more conservative dress, less talking and interruption in meetings, and more courtesy shown to those present whether this includes offering refreshment or not accepting a phone call.

Managers vary in their willingness to listen at length and respond to non–work-related conversation from staff or inquire into their work and personal problems. Some managers prefer to deal with employees strictly through the chain of command, routing personal inquiries to others, even from immediate subordinates, who, if they have a drinking problem, may be referred to a human resources staff expert on substance abuse. Other managers keep their doors open, welcoming frequent interruptions and non-work questions.

Some managers prefer opulent or cluttered offices, others bare or sparsely furnished ones. Some managers place a large desk between themselves and visitors, sitting in an oversized swivel chair on a raised platform while their visitors have low chairs. Others have a worktable and no desk and meet with visitors in armchairs around a low coffee table.

There is generally no right or wrong answer to a question of management style. Within a wide range of the acceptable, style may not significantly affect managerial job performance. Certain styles fit better in certain organizations. It is safe to assume, however, in most large health services organizations anyway, that managers should dress conservatively, show courtesy to clinicians, and listen and give the appearance of listening, especially when addressed by persons who think they have higher status. Different stakeholders in an organization expect managers to behave in different ways, and managers should attempt to understand such expectations. Many managers tune in to others' needs better than other employees and have been selected for their jobs at least in part because their style better fits the expectations of those who have done the selecting.

The manager's style can set a tone for the entire organization and is often a focus of staff attention. For example, if the manager is open, trusting, and supportive while being professional and demanding, others in key organizational roles may tend to behave likewise.

Personality

Personality is an important aspect of the way managers are perceived, or whether they are trusted. Personality can have a significant impact on managerial effectiveness and survival. Of course, different stakeholders have different ideas about what is pleasant.

For example, a boss can have tremendous ability and intelligence, be friendly, cheerful, enthusiastic, witty, and appear open. Yet he may also have an enormous ego and be dishonest, hot-tempered, and inconsiderate. This executive may read staff mail and insist that staff never close their office doors. He may inspire in employees a determination to do only what he specifically requests—and to look out for themselves rather than for the boss's interest or the organization's. Yet this executive may be successful in meeting the demands of superiors and in attracting and retaining competent staff.

Another boss may be able, friendly, cheerful, open, witty, honest, considerate, intelligent, and calm. If she has a big ego, it is concealed in everyday relations. This boss obtains the resources necessary for staff to accomplish their work and is always available to help with a job-related or personal problem. The staff's response may be to do anything this manager asks and to give much higher priority to her concerns and the organization's. Yet this manager may be perceived by other stakeholders as cold, ruthless, and insufficiently concerned with their interests.

It is difficult for some managers to see themselves as others see them. Sometimes only friends, when not discouraged, will be appropriately critical. Friends may be wrong about a question at issue, but they are less likely to be wrong about how others perceive the manager. Generally coworkers, especially subordinates, do not volunteer negative criticism because they have an interest in saying what they think the manager wants to hear. Some wait for the manager to be in a relaxed mood before sharing concerns. If the manager is always on the go, he may never be perceived as being in the mood to listen to such feedback. Subordinates may feel unsure in their assessments or wish to give the manager the benefit of the doubt. Managers need to get open feedback from staff about their feelings and perceptions prior to communicating on important issues with key stakeholders.

Managers should not attempt to change their style merely because they see other styles working better for other managers. Often such change is not easily accomplished and, if forced, leads to worse or different results than intended. Managers should know themselves, however, and what it is about themselves that key stakeholders like or dislike. In this way, managers can better adapt to the demands of a situation, take advantage of what they have going for them, and allow for or minimize weak points, for example, through delegation or by being joined at an important meeting by another staff member who has strengths the manager lacks.

MANAGING YOUR EDUCATION

What kinds of skills and experience do you need to become an effective health services manager? What skills and experience are best learned on the job or through formal educational programs? What type of formal educational program should an aspiring health services manager pursue during her career?

Richard Boyatzis has subdivided management into 22 abilities and 11 knowledge areas.[13] The abilities are subdivided into three groups: goals and action management, people management, and analytical reasoning, listed as follows:

Goal and Action Management Abilities

1. Efficiency orientation
2. Planning
3. Initiative
4. Attention to detail
5. Self-control
6. Flexibility

People Management Abilities

7. Empathy
8. Persuasiveness
9. Networking
10. Negotiating
11. Self-confidence

12. Group management
13. Developing others
14. Oral communication

Analytical Reasoning Abilities

15. Use of concepts
16. Systems thinking
17. Pattern recognition
18. Theory building
19. Using technology
20. Quantitative analysis
21. Social objectivity
22. Written communication

The knowledge areas are as follows:

1. Accounting
2. Banking and finance
3. Economics
4. Labor and human resource policy
5. Marketing
6. Management information and decision systems
7. Operations research
8. Operations management
9. Organizational behavior
10. Policy
11. Managerial statistics

Many of the knowledge areas can be applied more specifically to health-care or can be taught using healthcare examples (e.g., healthcare marketing). Additional knowledge areas specific to healthcare include:

12. Comparative systems
13. Payment systems and insurance

Of course, making such a list does not indicate how much one has to learn about a topic and whether it can best be learned on the job or at school.

Graduate programs offer a number of required and elective courses to train competent health service managers, often using health examples to apply disciplinary or multidisciplinary content. Graduate programs have different philosophies that underlie their curriculum. A discussion with faculty and students and a review of mission and curriculum can be helpful in choosing which program to attend.

What follows is our advice to someone asking about the formal education required to obtain a managerial job in healthcare. First, get a good education at high school (learn how to read and write), and at college major in the social sciences. During the process get work experience, particularly that which involves managing something (e.g., managing your school team or newspaper). After college, get a job in a healthcare organization in or with management, and work there for two or three years. Next go to an accredited graduate program, most of which are in schools of business, public health, or public administration (all of whose curricula must meet the same accreditation criteria). You can get a list of the more than 60 accredited graduate programs from the Association of University Programs in Health Administration, 730 11th street NW, 4th floor, Washington, D.C. Then, after the master's, start work in a large health services organization, where a broad range of experience and contacts are available (for someone with little experience, it may be preferable to start out in a smaller, less daunting organization). While there, plan out your next position and how to get there, and keep learning. Try to develop a special area of competence within health services management, such as finance, information services, or marketing.

Common problems and concerns the authors find in trying to assist and coach our own graduate students include: students who lack managerial experience and clinicians seeking management careers on a part-time basis who retain the mind-set of clinicians rather than of managers. In the job market, students seem to do well at responding to change and repackaging themselves accordingly while at school, through part-time jobs and elective courses. With regard to the first group, we suggest that healthcare management programs require at least two years of work experience (as do those programs located in many business schools) before students are accepted into the program. Regarding the clinicians, we suspect that some should not enroll, or be accepted, in management programs, as they will find management not really to their interest relative to other career opportunities.

Some argue that managers are born and not made and that managers can become CEOs or assistant administrators without a graduate degree. Rather than a more or less liberal education, prospective managers do pursue an undergraduate education in health services management. They go to graduate school right from college and they attend graduate programs that are not unaccredited. We strongly urge those considering these decisions to seek the advice of managers who work in healthcare organizations, and of students who attend the accredited graduate programs.

Arguments that have been made for first pursuing an undergraduate degree in health services management include that the individual already knows the career that she wants to pursue, that she can get a graduate degree faster (in a combined program) or can learn more in graduate school by waiving some courses, or that she doesn't need graduate education at all because she can learn what she needs to know on the job or through special shorter educational programs. We don't agree. Many managerial job descriptions require the master's degree and many managers with such degrees find this an appropriate job requirement.

The argument for going straight from college to grad school is that it may be easier to be admitted immediately after college, and going to school may be easier immediately after college, especially if school can be financed with scholarships and part-time work. An unaccredited graduate program may be all that is available in a certain locality and may be even easier to get admitted to and be cheaper and shorter than an accredited program.

When evaluating a graduate program, applicants should consider the following criteria: quality and quantity of the faculty; emphasis on teaching in the program relative to other activities; commitment of the faculty to student advising; the depth, breadth, and relevance of the curriculum; the realistic availability of field experience and post-graduate placement services; student participation in decision making; help in financing and planning the financing of education; and an active, supportive alumni association. Personal criteria may include school location, availability of financial aid and part-time work, length of the curriculum, scheduling of classes, cost, availability of student housing, and probability of admission. Students may be interested in cultural diversity of the student body and the faculty either because they are members of minority groups or prefer a culturally diverse setting. Visits to classes and conversations with recent alumni and faculty can help prospective applicants make a more informed choice.

3
Managerial Contribution to Effective Performance

My job is neither to control the members personally nor to run their affairs, but it is to be able to put those tigers on the stools so the act will be performed, and when a tiger is off the stool, I have to find him and get him back on the stool, or the people will want their money back.

— John Danielson, former hospital CEO

THERE CAN BE LITTLE AGREEMENT ABOUT managerial contribution to effective performance unless there is prior agreement on the definition of "effective performance." This may be defined in terms of the measurable objectives of the organization, as related to the organization's mission and goals, or in terms of the goals of key stakeholders, those who provide the organization with resources. The point of view that will be taken here is that organizations are temporary organizations that are provided with resources by society so long as they add sufficient value to these inputs to generate a greater return than if the resources were provided elsewhere. The goals of the organization are set in measurable terms in advance of a time period, then shared with key stakeholders and amended, taking into consideration stakeholder expectations. Then progress in meeting the objectives is reported regularly to owners and stakeholders, and over time either objectives or strategies are changed to justify continued societal provision of resources to the organization to survive and grow. This obviously is a normative rather than a descriptive perspective as few, if any, organizations act in the manner prescribed. What this perspective does present is a framework for viewing organizational performance and managerial contribution that can be valuable in considering proposed action. Such a framework can only be constructed after current circumstances are accurately viewed with regard to the organization's performance and managerial contribution and after problems and issues are considered and changes in objectives and strategies suggested that are realistic, in terms of required resources, and aligned, in terms of the interests of those in positions of authority and power.

MEASURING ORGANIZATIONAL PERFORMANCE

One reason for attempting to specify effective or acceptable organizational performance is to focus attention on who "owns" the organization. If performance is acceptable to managers, physicians, and trustees, does it matter what anyone else thinks? If it does matter, what are others going to do if they find performance unacceptable?

Another reason for developing measures of organizational performance has to do with the distribution of organizational resources. To adjudicate claims on resources among key groups and individuals, questions arise about the organization's purposes. For example, "What is the organization doing? How does what we do compare to what our competitors do? How does what we do compare with what our physicians, nurses, staff, trustees, customers, and potential customers think we ought to be doing?"

Prior agreement about standards of performance facilitates agreement on performance evaluation; otherwise, performance would not be measurable in terms such as "excellent," "acceptable," and "unacceptable." Statements such as "the HMO operated at $100,000 surplus this year," "one percent of patients made formal complaints," and "our turnover rate in nursing decreased to 15 percent this year" are uncertain indicators of performance unless they can be related to agreed-on

Figure 3.1   Dimensions of Healthcare Measures

Input-Oriented	Output-Oriented
Demand	*Outputs*
Patient management	Treatments
Clinical management	Productivity
Logistic management	
Cost/Resources	*Quality*
Costs	Clinical outcomes
Physical counts	Patient satisfaction
Resource condition	Procedural quality
Human Resources	*Revenue*
Worker/physician	Profit
Satisfaction	Implicit price
Supply	

Source: Griffith, J.R., V.K. Sahney, and R.A. Mohr. 1995. *Reengineering Health Care*. Chicago: Health Administration Press.

standards and purposes. The standards of performance for which the organization and its managers are to be held accountable must be made clear in advance.

PUTTING PERFORMANCE REQUIREMENTS INTO OPERATION

Standards can be developed regarding dimensions of healthcare that are input-oriented and output-oriented (see Figure 3.1 as developed by Griffith, Sahney, and Mohr 1995). Information systems must track these dimensions.

Intermountain Health Care had an explicit plan for information improvement as of 1995 that is outlined in Exhibit 3.1. Indicators can be quantified in terms of desired changes rather than points of performance. Certain indicators, such as financial ratios, are easier to quantify than, say, the commitment of physicians and nurses to organizational performance requirements. Yet commitment can be quantified in terms of turnover and absenteeism rates; unit costs per clinical service relative to industry standards; nurses' attitudes as measured by

Exhibit 3.1

Plan for Information Improvement at IHC

CQI Measurement—Current and Future

	Recipient			Customer Service		Clinical Quality	Finance
IHC	Cluster	Hosp	Freq				
CURRENT				Nonmedical Outcomes	Satisfaction	Medical Outcomes	Cost per Case
				• Inpatient admissions • Outpatient registrations • Average inpatient age • Average length of stay • Case mix index	• Perceptions of overall hospital quality • Perceptions of hospital staff • Perceptions of clinical process and outcomes	• Mortality • Infection rates • Repeats and returns to O.R. • Adverse drug reactions	• Net operating income • Controllable expense variance • Charge per case (CMI-adj) • Medicare charge per case
FUTURE				Process	Satisfaction/Expectation	Medical Outcomes	Cost per Case
				• Patient delays and waiting times • Forms per patient • Person-hours per STAT (efficiency) • Number of processes analyzed	• Referral and hold rates (MDs/clinics) • Employee retention and turnover rates • Satisfaction by dept. and specialization • Expectation profiles and patterns	• Injuries • Severity indices • Functional status • Cure rates • Complication rates • Readmits • Long-term clinical outcomes	• Uniform cost per case (adjusted for severity) • Uncompensated care • Cost per day of stay • Volumes

Source: Intermountain Health Care System. 1995.

surveys; physician behavior as measured by attendance at organizational social functions and financial contributions to fund-raising campaigns. Whether the effort and cost of putting such requirements into operation is worth it or whether these are right or best measures, are, of course, separate and not trivial questions.

REASONS FOR NOT SPECIFYING OBJECTIVES

One of the difficulties in measuring organizational performance is the very concept of performance objectives. Perrow has argued that the concept of organizational goals as a major influence on organizational behavior is "only a convenient fiction" and that much of what happens in organizations results from

> …happenstance, accidents, misunderstandings, and even random, un-motivated behavior…. Programs are started for a variety of vague and conflicting reasons, with the help of a lot of trivial or even accidental events…. Decision makers do not look for optimal solutions, have trouble discovering what they want, and settle for the first acceptable solution that comes along, which is usually what the organization has been doing. That is, they settle so long as some important person or group doesn't want to change what the organization is doing and how the organization has been doing it.[14]

Goal specification may not be necessary to achieving acceptable performance results in some organizations, at least not in the eyes of major contributors of resources. Specification costs may be high in relation to projected benefits, and it may be easier to accommodate diverse interests if goals are not specified. Competing members of a coalition may rarely see conflict among organizational objectives until goals are specified, at which time they may be forced to recognize and deal with the conflict. It may be easier to shift organizational direction if the proposed change does not have to meet criteria that have been previously defined and agreed to. Finally, board members, managers, and physicians may choose not to specify goals to avoid accountability and to maximize discretion or authority.

RESULTS OF NOT SPECIFYING GOALS

Not specifying or targeting organizational performance objectives are believed to result in lower levels of performance than would otherwise occur. By not focusing on which goals to attain, the organization may fail to attain them. Strong members of a coalition may gain more power or resources at the expense of weak members than they would have if the goals of the weak members had been considered formally by all participants. Short-run interests of a controlling coalition tend to be favored at the expense of the long-run interests of other stakeholders and potential stakeholders.

Long-term maintenance of organizational systems (that is, survival) may be threatened or short-term organizational crises may become more frequent and more severe when performance requirements are not specified and opportunistic interests prevail.

Without such specification, it may become more difficult to make and implement policy decisions—that is, to the extent that there is disagreement regarding effective performance requirements among the controlling coalition.

Not specifying performance requirements favors retention of the present power structure. The status quo will tend to be perceived as a satisfactory level of goal attainment as long as the organization can continue to obtain necessary and appropriate inputs and sell or dispose of adequate quantities of outputs.

The environment that many health services organizations face now is competitive, problematic, and changing rapidly. Interest groups within these organizations contest for resources, in which case specification of organizational objectives may be seen as less costly than direct conflict over limited resources. Evidence of a trend in this direction is found in the growth of large national health services corporations, which— at least, in the case of for-profit organizations—have well-developed internal systems specifying performance requirements by unit or department. Such internal systems are also characteristics of large community care organizations such as Henry Ford Health System and Intermountain Health Care. Organizations that have embraced continuous quality improvement (CQI) philosophy have focused attention and energy on goal congruence for all who work in the organization.

MEASURING MANAGERIAL CONTRIBUTION

If there is a lack of agreement as to how or whether the performance of health services organizations should be evaluated, there must obviously be a similar lack of agreement as to how or whether the managerial performance of these organizations should be evaluated.

It is difficult to isolate the managerial contribution to organizational performance. Despite substantial managerial contribution, an organization may be floundering because of a hostile environment or poor decisions by previous managers. Or the reverse may occur—despite little or ineffective managerial contribution, an organization may be growing rapidly or raising quality standards and performance because of a lack of competitors or excellent management in the past and excellent physicians and nurses at the present time.

REASONS FOR EVALUATING MANAGERS

Reasons for evaluating health services managers include the following:

- to avoid setting managers apart from all other employees, who are regularly evaluated;
- to determine continued employment and terms of employment;
- to set prospectively agreed-on managerial performance requirements and to assess how these requirements may be accomplished;
- to force self-examination in regard to managerial performance and improvements that would enhance it; and
- to provide a rationale for whatever the employer wants the manager to do or for whatever the manager has done or wants to do.

A manager may be evaluated relative to what he has accomplished previously or relative to what managers in similar organizations contribute, assuming a correlation between organizational and managerial performance.

THE EFFECTIVE HEALTH SERVICES MANAGER: HOW CAN YOU TELL?

The effective manager does what she is supposed to do. This can be further specified in terms of stakeholder analysis; she does what the key stakeholders expect (she knows who they are). So, what happens when key stakeholders do not agree? And what happens when the manager cannot do what the stakeholders expect (perhaps through no fault of her own)? To what extent can she influence stakeholder expectations so that these are appropriate?

Part of being an effective manager is figuring out a definition of what effectiveness in the job means and validating this view with key stakeholders. Typically, this involves deciding what work the manager is doing that shouldn't be done and which work should be done by somebody else. This assumes some vision of where the key stakeholders want the organization to be at the end of a certain period of time, as related to where they think the organization is now. There is something to be said here for the manager telling the key stakeholders who hired her before she accepts the job what it is she intends to do and how she intends to do it. This means in turn that a prospective manager is willing *not* to take the job if stakeholders do not agree.

Differentiating some effective managers from some ineffective managers whom the authors have personally worked with and observed, we would draw the following conclusions. Rather than varying in contribution to organizational performance, they seem to vary primarily with regard to personality. Three effective managers with whom one of us worked were all even-tempered, fair, and consistent; their management style consisted in reaching agreement as to what was expected, empowering subordinates and colleagues to do what was expected, getting them the resources needed to do the job, and giving them support should difficulties arise. Three ineffective managers were either hot-tempered, inconsistent, or both. Two of them directed one of the authors to do what they wanted done, then closely supervised my work; the third talked indirectly, depending on me to specify what it was that I was going to do, but refusing to be pinned down as to exactly what he wanted done or how he wanted it done. With the first two ineffective managers, I could never do the job as well as they could do it, and they saw their job as teaching me how to do the job right. With the third, everything was fine so long as no one complained; if that occurred, then I was confronted with the complaint and expected to rectify the matter. Their behavior relates to low competence on Goleman's emotional intelligence IQs, particularly in the areas of self-regulation, empathy, and social skills.[15]

In another book one of the authors said that what makes for an effective manager relates to the congruence between the choices the manager makes regarding the episodes of work he manages and how much time he chooses to spend on which episodes.[16] Also important are what kinds of results are produced relative to that effort, the congruence between the episodes managed, and the objectives and strategies of key stakeholders. That is, the assumption is made that the organization has articulated goals and objectives, and that judgment is made not according to outcomes, which may not be within the manager's control, but according to the processes he engages in. What matters is not only how well the manager plays his cards, but also which cards he is dealt.

Currently, we are drawn more to a concept of managerial effectiveness that is about a relationship between a manager and a job, rather than a concept inherent in any managerial performance per se. The same manager may be very effective in one situation and very ineffective in another. A key differentiator of effective and ineffective managers is integrity, meaning the manager is trusted and consistent. This leads to the conclusion that managers in pursuit of effectiveness need to spend much more time evaluating the fit between their skills and experience and validating what a particular job requires. One way to do this is to understand the success of the previous job occupant (and what this depended on), determine how his skills and experience resemble the prospective manager's, and estimate whether the job is the same or how it has changed.

If the manager makes a mistake in the choice of a job, there is no reason to stay in the job and perpetuate the bad choice. In this light, it is important for managers to figure out in advance how to know whether the job is not working out and to have an exit strategy toward doing something else. There is always a good chance that the manager will not be the right person for the job even if the employer and the manager think that she is the right person. At the least, the job requirements may change or the boss or a key subordinate or colleague may change.

The key here is leaving when the manager can be in control of her departure rather than when those who hired her want her gone. Our impression is that those who hired the manager will be much more supportive and generous in calling it quits (or in changing their own behavior) when the manager says to them, at the right time, in the right place, in the right tone, "I don't think the job is working out. I'm doing the best that I can and will continue to do the best that I can, but I will need a little time to find another position." Hopefully, the manager will already be deep in search for another position before she initiates this conversation. What if there is no position, or no suitable position? Well, the manager would be leaving anyway; her employer wants her to do certain tasks, and either she cannot do them or she doesn't think she ought to be doing them. This is the kind of thinking managers need to go through before accepting a job in the first instance.

THE MANAGER'S PERSPECTIVE

Just as managers have a responsibility to formally evaluate subordinates who are accountable to them for performance, they should desire a formal evaluation of their own performance. If the purpose of the evaluation is to assist managers to improve performance, then they should participate actively in the process. Evaluation should be a continuing iterative process that is flexible enough to take into account internal and external forces constraining and facilitating performance.

The evaluation process is time consuming, especially the first time. Trustees, managers, and department heads undoubtedly feel uncomfortable about an initial evaluation, whether they are being evaluated or whether they are evaluating others. The measures used may have limited validity and reliability. If the evaluation results do not square with the manager's own judgment, the cause may be faulty measurement tools or measurement bias, not necessarily the manager's faulty judgment.

EVALUATING THE INDIVIDUAL MANAGER

One approach to managerial evaluation that one of the authors helped develop as a manager begins with specifying key aspects of a top manager's job; a similar evaluation approach is detailed by Michael Rindler.[17] These specifications are developed both by the manager and a board committee. Six to twelve months later, the manager and the committee separately evaluate managerial performance. In the case of a lower-level manager, the evaluation process is developed jointly by a superior and a subordinate in relation to written guidelines. There are at least three levels of performance—excellent, acceptable, and unacceptable—and an opportunity for noting strong points or areas needing improvement in each aspect of performance.

After meeting without the manager present, the board committee summarizes its judgment and indicates to the manager the areas in which the committee agrees or disagrees with the manager's own evaluation. Then they meet together to review ways of improving managerial performance and of improving the evaluation process. The manager and the chairs of the committee sign what they have agreed to, indicating any remaining areas of disagreement and any agreement as to future plans and recommendations. The manager's evaluation is then used as an important input into superiors' decisions regarding salary and tenure. The evaluation process is confidential, as are all employee performance evaluations. Of course, this rational approach can be at variance with the underlying reality, which may be primarily political relative to the interests of respective stakeholders. Formal evaluation of a chief executive officer is done at least annually for the first few years of an appointment and again at least several months before any renewal or termination of a longer-term contract.

A related evaluation approach for middle management is shown in Exhibit 3.2. The form relates results to job description and previous goal statements. Examples of present performance must be specified in ratings other than "good." Mutually formulated goals are requested for a future period, and the evaluator is asked to identify special efforts that will be made to assist the employee to achieve these goals. Employee comments and signatures are asked for, as are requests for future assignment to other positions within the organization or system.

Exhibit 3.2   Sample Management Supervisory Development Evaluation

Employee's Name: Janet Rouse   Position/Title   VP Facilities

Department: Adminstration   Date Prepared: 8/7/92 Date of Hire: 7/1/84

Period covered by Evaluation: From: 7/1/91   To: 6/30/92

Development Factors and Evaluation	Examples of Present Performance Rating (necessary if rated other than good)
I. *Results:* In relationship to job description and previous goal statements.	Actions for the last year demonstrate a new level of job interest and enthusiasm. Completed upgrade of the OR air handling system on time and with minimal disruption. Excellent work in improving department head understanding of management information systems and budget reports yielding cost reduction of $200,000.
II. *Job Knowledge:* How has current level of technical/professional/specialist knowledge affected overall results?	Knowledge of building and its systems has grown plus development of operating manuals to ensure continuity of services.
III. *Quantity of Work:* As compared to others under your direction, as compared to optimum level desired, as compared against previous periods of time.	Level of activity is commensurate with position. Focus more on job responsibilities, not those of others.
IV. *Quality of Work:* As compared to others under your direction, as compared to optimum level desired, as compared against previous periods of time.	Quality of work shows improvement. Beginning to show strengths to her peers which had not always been obvious.
V. *Financial Responsibility:* How have dollars budgeted been managed? Have unfavorable variances been justified by results?	Tendency to make decisions which have short-term savings, but higher costs over the long run. The use of a low-cost maintenance firm for the chillers resulted in a possibly unnecessary $55,000 expenditure.

Exhibit 3.2 Continued

Development Factors and Evaluation	Examples of Present Performance Rating
VI. *Personnel Responsibility:* Consider examples of staff development, delegation, discipline, grievances, turnover, teamwork, and results generated by staff under person's direction.	Stable department heads. The results from using Total Quality Management (TQM) techniques within the division have been quite noticeable.
VII. *Dependability:* Consider meeting of deadlines, completion of work, attendance, punctuality, and follow-up on areas of responsibility.	Continues to put in long days with meeting her deadlines and obligations consistently.
VIII. *Communications:* Consider verbal and written skills and results achieved.	Tendency to speak before thinking of the implications of her words.
IX. *Leadership and Initiative:* How effectively and in what situations has this person "taken charge"? What are the results?	Takes charge and follows it with action. Consider doing this in a calm and deliberate fashion.
X. *Cooperation:* Consider how working relationships with supervisors, peers, and staff have affected results.	Good channel of information to medical staff. Good relationships with peers and other staff.
XI. *Planning:* How has this person prepared personally the staff and the sphere of responsibility for the future: are plans prepared?	Area that needs greater attention. Good quality work achieved, could be excellent with better planning.
XII. *Special Factor:* Specific Goals for Future Period (Mutually Formulated)	*Evaluator Statement of Commitment* (Identify specific efforts that you will engage in to assist employee to achieve the specific goals referenced during the coming period)
Expand the TQM process to two more departments and three new teams.	Provide release time to the staff to participate in the TQM process.
Develop a control process for work orders that includes skill mix and total costs.	Provide support for computer-generated records.

Continued

Exhibit 3.2 Continued

Prepared by: Jason Weill   Position Title: Senior VicePresident/COO

Reviewed by: Edgar Kayce   Position Title: President

Date discussed with employee: 8/14/92

Employee comments:

I have learned a great deal in this area of the hospital and am looking forward to taking on the role of clinical responsibility and work closer with the medical staff. I am particularly interested in program development and new business opportunities. As you know, I took two marketing courses this past year.

This past year has been a real growing experience for me. I believe I have made significant progress with the operations I directed. The cost savings to the hospital were significant, and made a difference to the staff. I am looking to take on new responsibilities.

Employee Signature: _____   Date: _____

INCENTIVE COMPENSATION PROGRAMS

Incentive compensation programs for managers are becoming increasingly more common. These can be administered on a group basis or individually. Through profit or surplus sharing, such incentive programs can be part of every employee's compensation package. For managers, typically, the incentive compensation package is tied to a set of goals and objectives developed between the manager and the manager's superiors, whether this is the board or a senior manager. Clearly the more precisely a goal can be specified, the more realistic it is to have an element of compensation tied to it.

One difficulty is how to define these arrangements for top managers when many activities are process oriented and of limited short-term outcome orientation. The risk is always there that managers will attempt to set objectives too low or to "cook the numbers," as creative accounting can move those numbers in a desired direction.

Should incentive compensation be implemented regarding top management, consideration should be given to implementing a similar program for all employees. This approach requires a significant investment in time and effort to produce a plan that is consistent with organizational mission and goals and acceptable to employees. An advantage of profit or surplus sharing is that base pay can be set a bit lower than otherwise might be the case, locking in a margin of safety should performance fail to meet the targets and yet ensuring financial surplus sharing should targets be met or exceeded. Of course, there are costs in setting up and administering the process, and conflicts engendered regarding the setting of targets for performance and related financial rewards.

PRACTICAL PROBLEMS WITH PERFORMANCE APPRAISALS

Andrew Grove,[18] a believer in effective performance appraisal, has indicated the following problems that occur in practice:

- Comments about subordinate performance are too general.
- The employee receives mixed messages when problems are mentioned but with no specifics concerning documentation or approaches to solutions.
- Negatives are avoided.
- The supervisor does not know the employee's work sufficiently well.
- Only recent performance is considered.
- The report is a surprise to the employee.
- The evaluator is not formally accountable for the quality of the appraisal.

Deming has suggested that performance appraisals lack validity when individual managers lack control over the outcomes of their work.[19] Given the difficulty of agreeing on outcomes and validity of methods, perhaps the greatest benefit of appraising performance is the resultant clarity in expectations among the parties to the appraisal and any insights generated from focusing on managerial contribution.

4

Finding Your Niche

Administration in a very large hospital is an entirely different problem from management of a small institution, and the very characteristics which would make for success in the former might become a handicap in the latter.

— Malcolm MacEachern, *Hospital Organization and Management*, 1947*

HEALTH SERVICES MANAGERS SHOULD MANAGE their careers just as they manage their work on the job. In this chapter, we first discuss job opportunities in health services management and terms of employment; we go on to cover getting a first job, changing career direction or improving the present situation; finally, we present other career options related to health services management.

WHAT IS AVAILABLE

The field is vast. Health services managers are involved in general management, financial management, strategic planning, human resources management, program development and evaluation, management information systems, marketing, and operations and policy analysis. Managers operate service programs for community groups,

---

*Dr. MacEachern has been called the father of health services management, writing the "Bible" on hospital organization and management in 1935, in which he is referred to in one of six introductions as "this distinguished director of Hospital Standardization of the American College of Surgeons, having spent a life time in the study and direction of hospitals, visiting more hospitals, meeting more of their administrators, consulting on more hospital problems than any man in or out of the hospital field."

gather information for compliance with governmental regulations for large health services corporations, arbitrate and mediate among different health occupations and groups concerning the allocation of scarce resources, and assist in generating revenues for a variety of organizations.

Health services managers are employed by organizations that vary in size from the group practice with five physicians to the large health-care system with more than 90,000 non-physician employees and more than 9,000 physicians, national in scope and operating in states in which most Americans live. Organizations that employ health services managers include hospitals and health systems, nursing homes, health maintenance organizations (HMOs) and other insurance companies, group practices, neighborhood health centers, home care agencies, ambulatory surgery centers, medical day care programs, durable equipment companies, home infusion agencies, and hospices.

Various interests sponsor or own health services organizations, including local community groups, federal, state, and local governments, unions, business corporations (investor-owned or other), cooperatives, and physicians and other professionals. Hundreds of thousands of management positions are available in patient care management, support services, and for-profit organizations that sell to or buy from health services organizations.

As of 1999, the overall employment situation remains good for candidates with the requisite skills and experience. Not everyone seeking positions will find exactly the job he is looking for, as certain parts of the industry, or geographic areas, are characterized by supply in excess of demand, while the reverse is true for other sectors and areas.

Typical positions for a recent graduate from a master's program in health services management in 1998 include the following:

- Associate, Healthcare Consulting firm
- Decision Support Analyst, Medical Center
- Partnership Manager, HMO
- Compliance Officer, Insurance Company
- Business Manager, Emergency Medicine
- Planning Analyst, Nonprofit Hospital

- Assistant Administrator, Small Rural Hospital
- Organizational Performance Coordinator, Medical Center
- Manager, Clinical Department

TERMS OF EMPLOYMENT

Terms of employment may include pay, benefits, additional income, managerial contracts, and policies regarding conflicts of interest. Most important terms may not be validly quantified. Examples include working in a growing organization, the opportunity to learn, and the support of a senior manager who is interested in developing the manager's career.

Pay

Managerial salaries in healthcare vary by organization, area of the country, managerial level, functional area, and financial performance of the organization. According to a management compensation survey conducted in 1996 of 241 participating organizations (including 73 integrated delivery system headquarters, 601 hospitals, 14 long-term care facilities, 7 managed care organizations, 7 home health agencies, 15 physician groups, and 15 sub-acute ambulatory care facilities), the median total compensation for the administrator/chief executive officer for all hospitals was $195,600. The number eligible to receive a bonus of some sort is 375 out of 455 surveyed, or 82 percent. The average bonus is 40 percent of base salary.[20] Starting salaries for graduates of one master's program ranged from $35,000 to $40,000 for graduates with minimum experience.

In business organizations, it is not uncommon for 50 percent of total compensation for the top manager and 10 to 25 percent for middle managers to be based on incentive pay relative to financial and other annual targets. Bonuses may be company-wide and based on company, or unit/department-based and based on local performance, or individually based on job position. In any case, the organization budgets for a pool of assets to cover bonuses, bases individual awards on achievement of objectives, and specifies maximum awards that can be achieved.

Benefits

Manager benefits can be substantial, particularly in large organizations, usually ranging from 20 to 30 percent of salary. Hospitalization and medical care benefits are usually the same for all employees, although the amount of other benefits, such as insurance, will vary with job classification and salary.

The list of benefits that certain managers can obtain is long. This includes auto and related expenses, housing, entertainment, travel, membership dues in country clubs, and, for a few, private school tuition for children. Almost any living expense can be viewed as a job-related expense because managers can always be working at home or while traveling. Managers may be talking to people who can help the organization during most of their waking hours. In that case, it may benefit the organization to pay others to drive the manager to work or do their banking. Some managers regard as benefits the size and furnishing of their offices and the number and pay of their assistants.

Additional Income

Most health services managers can increase their pay only through promotions, cost-of-living raises, and bonuses. Occasionally a job can be reclassified as a result of changes in responsibility, duties, and organizational change, or pay for the job can be reclassified because of a change in competitive conditions (or a job offer).

If the manager is greatly in need of additional income, some managers pursue alternative sources of revenue. If this is in the form of a job, it is generally wise that managers clear this with their employer; most employers will not approve. It is conceivable that in some smaller organizations, functional managers in particular may change their employment status from employee to consultant, thereby losing benefits but enabling them to take a similar job as consultant for a similar organization. Alternatively, the manager may choose to spend fewer hours at the job and more hours at home, thereby enabling a spouse or partner to earn additional income.

By special arrangement with an employer, the manager can teach or consult in the evenings, on weekends, or for a fixed amount of time during regular working hours. Most employers insist on approving such activities in advance, in which case an agreement would have to be reached as to whether the manager may keep any funds generated from such activities or whether the funds must be returned to offset the manager's salary.

Management Contracts

Management contracts are legal agreements for ensuring tenure in a particular position for a specified period of time. Increasingly common, they are important for top managers (they are less common for other managers). Among the purposes of these contracts are recruiting and protecting the manager and encouraging managerial initiative. A contract does not prevent the chief executive officer from being fired quickly by the board, but it raises the cost of firing the CEO. For a sample management contract, see Appendix A.

Management contracts are virtually unenforceable from the employer's side because the board cannot force a manager to manage. Nor can the organization keep a manager from leaving. However, the contract may limit the manager's choice of new employers.

Conflicts of Interest

Conflict of interest is usually related to managerial decisions being affected by special interests in return for gifts or favors. Conflicts of interest can involve decisions concerning the income and expense of those who work in an organization, sell to an organization, or use the organization's services. For example, a supplier may ask the manager out to dinner or to a ball game to get a contract. The situation may be acceptable if it is a meal at a local restaurant, but not if it is a weekend in Hawaii. Managers may wish to steer certain organizational purchases, such as insurance, to friends and relatives. Board members may wish to steer banking or telephone business to their bank or telephone company.

Managers can rationalize acting in conflict with the organization's interest by choosing not to see the conflict, arguing that "everyone else does it" or that the manager will not get caught, or pretending that it does not make any difference. It does make a difference, however, in terms of how the manager is perceived and therefore in what the manager can expect from those who are accountable to her. We can think of no case in which the gain of steering a contract is worth the potential cost.

Section II.C of the American College of Healthcare Executives *Code of Ethics* deals with conflicts of interest (see Appendix B).

GETTING A FIRST JOB

The basic process of getting a first job involves assessing skills, experience, and managerial preferences as related to jobs available. Of course, it helps to have planned for this before actually seeking a first job in health services management—that is, through education and other employment. Management students can test out their ideas about employment with faculty advisors, residency preceptors, guest lecturers, the program director, fellow students, and the school placement office. Remember that placement is the manager's responsibility, not that of school officials.

Talk with alumni of the school. Get advice from managers who hold positions of interest. What do they like and dislike about their jobs? How do they spend their time? How are their jobs changing? What do they need to know to be able to do their jobs well? How did they decide what they wanted to do? Has it worked out for them the way they expected? What are the skills and experience required to obtain the kind of job they now have? In the process of seeking advice, the job-seeker may find a manager who will teach her or help her, or who may even hire her or recommend her to another potential employer.

The student can identify managers who hold positions similar to the ones the student is interested in obtaining and ask friends, teachers, and others to identify people for "informational interviews." During two years of study in a graduate program, students will be exposed to a variety of role models. Many managers whom students wish to meet will be pleased to help them. Student interest is flattering to managers who like their work and who like themselves. Time required for such meetings is modest. Student questions may cause even experienced managers to rethink certain problems or learn from saying things that surprise themselves.

WHAT ARE EMPLOYERS LOOKING FOR?

Employers want to hire team players who can help the organization
and who will make their supervisors look good—that is, someone who
is going to work hard and smart and not irritate important stakeholders. For most entry-level managerial jobs, managers have to be enthusiastic about listening, absorb a great deal of information, and communicate to others what they mean in a clear and non-threatening
way. These tasks will be easier to accomplish if managers have a clear
understanding of their own strengths and weaknesses. Working effectively with others is difficult when managers do not know how others
see them. Working effectively is a function of wanting to succeed, of
focusing on a particular job's requirements, or being physically and
mentally fit. Not irritating others is a function of the manager's liking
himself, of not having to prove something, of enjoying people for themselves, and of respecting differences.

What does the job seeker say if his resume shows no experience?
"To get experience, I have to start somewhere, which is why I am
applying for this job" or "I have gone to school for a number of years;
in graduate school I have been exposed to these organizations and
these managers and have completed these projects. I can learn what I
need to know about working in your organization fairly quickly,
through orientation, observation, and discussions with peers, subordinates and superiors." The latter response is more likely to help the
candidate land the job.

Internships, residencies, and fellowships, while competitive, are
often easier to obtain than health services management positions. They
allow you to build experience, work on your network, and introduce
you to organizational sponsors. Many students are involved in internships on a voluntary basis, ones that demonstrate to an employer a
willingness to take on work. Volunteer work is a good way to demonstrate your accomplishments and motivation.

Job seekers must remember that although the competition will be
stiff, they are only looking for *one* job. The program graduate has been
able to complete demanding work at a good school, and if he works
hard and gets along with others, some employer will benefit from
the hire.

FINDING OUT WHERE THE JOBS ARE

Contact your friends in the field and tell them you are looking. Get in touch with your program director, faculty advisor, and school and professional organization placement offices. According to Jacob O. Victory, a recent program graduate, the school's alumni are the most helpful and the best source for information about jobs.[21] Search the Internet (see Chapter 10). Read the advertisements in local and national newspapers; in professional journals such as *Modern Healthcare, Hospitals,* the *Journal of the Medical Group Management Association,* and the *Journal of the American Public Health Association;* and in newsletters, such as those published by the American College of Healthcare Executives (ACHE) and the Medical Group Management Association. Members of ACHE can access the association's online Job Bank, a continuously updated nationwide listing of available executive positions.

GETTING AN INTERVIEW

To get a job interview, start by packaging your track record in a resume. This resume should be handsome but not extravagant in appearance; it must be clear and error-free, and it should indicate results and contributions, as appropriate, as well as skills and experience. Do not make your resume longer than two pages (one page, if you lack experience). For an example of a resume of a manager with considerable experience, see Exhibit 4.1. For an example of a resume of a less experienced manager, see Exhibit 4.2.

When the job seeker learns of an available position, he should try to establish personal contact with the person who will determine final applicants. Obviously, it helps to have established this contact before the job becomes available, or to know someone who knows the person with the final decision. Such contact is not always as impossible as it may seem; in larger organizations, entry-level managerial positions may turn over quickly; in expanding organizations, new positions are often created. Graduate program alumni often inform program directors, the placement office, and faculty when jobs become available.

Often it is not possible to establish personal contact with people who screen managerial applications (these may even be contracted

Exhibit 4.1   Resume of Experienced Manager

JOHN D. DOE, D.H.A., FACHE
President and CEO
Clara Maass Health System

Home Address
11 Park Place
Belleville, NJ 07109
(201) 000-0000

Business Address
One Clara Maass Drive
Belleville, NJ 07109
(201) 000-0000 Fax (201) 000-0000

LEADERSHIP PROFILE
Twenty-five years of progressive executive experience in diverse corporate environments. Career emphasis on optimizing individual and organizational performance. Extensive experience in pioneering and developing integrated delivery systems (IDS) and stakeholder partnerships where vision, leadership, and market understanding are essential. Professional reputation for developing and implementing strategic initiatives characterized by affordable, accessible, and quality programs and services.

PROFESSIONAL EXPERIENCE
President and CEO (1983–Present)
Clara Maass Health Systems and Medical Center, Belleville, New Jersey
Integrated delivery system (IDS) with $180 million annual revenue and 1,800 employees to include: 465-bed medical center, two nursing homes (302 beds), subacute, home health and hospice, imaging and ambulatory centers, PHO, and physician offices and practices.
- Restructured medical center into a holding company–controlled integrated health system.
- Established strategic planning process and implemented strategies that enhanced market share.
- Developed and implemented the most comprehensive continuum of health services in northern New Jersey.
- Defined roles and integrated board, management, and medical staff throughout the organization.
- Developed jointly operated physician-hospital organization (PHO) with more than 50 managed care contracts.
- Developed and completed two $30 million capital improvement and expansion projects.
- Maintained strong financial balance sheet and access to competitive capital rates.

Vice President (1977–1983)
North Carolina Baptist Hospitals, Winston-Salem, North Carolina
Major teaching hospital for Bowman Gray School of Medicine with more than 700 beds and 3,000 employees.
- Efficiently led patient care functions to include nursing services, central services, clinical laboratories, pharmacy, operating rooms. Scope of responsibilities included 1,700 employees and $80 million in revenue.
- Successfully integrated medical education and research into medical center programs and services.

Administrator (1975–1977)
Hospital Affiliates International (HAI), Nashville, Tennessee
National proprietary hospital chain.
- Fulfilled responsibilities and duties of Associate, Regional Assistant, and Administrator at owned and managed hospitals throughout the southeast.
- Successfully turned around Joint Commission and financial performance of 140-bed county-owned hospital.

Continued

Exhibit 4.1 Continued

Administrative Assistant (1973–1975)
Easton Hospital, Easton, Pennsylvania
- One of three administrators for 311-bed community teaching hospital.
- Assisted in management of day-to-day operations.
- Responsible for materials management, Joint Commission surveys and state inspections, housekeeping, medical records, and UR.

PROFESSIONAL AND CIVIC ORGANIZATIONS
- University Healthcare Corporation Board of Trustees (1994–Present)
- VHA East and New Jersey consolidated Board of Trustees (Present)
- New Jersey Hospital Association Board of Directors (1990–1996)
- Presbyterian Homes of New Jersey Board of Trustees (1992–1995)
- ACHE Management Series Editorial Board (1992–1995)
- Essex/Hudson/Union Counties Hospital Administration Council Chair (1991–1993)
- ACHE Committee on Ethics (1989–1992)
- ACHE Fellow

FACULTY APPOINTMENTS
- New York University Graduate School of Public Service, Visiting Faculty (1995–1996)
- Washington University, Adjunct Faculty (1996–1997)

PUBLICATIONS
- *Health Services Management*, 5th ed., edited by A.R. Kovner, and D. Neuhauser, contributing author, Fall, 1997
- "Integrating the Physician into the Organization Decision-Making Process," *Best Practices and Benchmarking in Healthcare*, January/February 1996, co-author.
- "Opening Additional Hospital Beds During an Acute Nursing Shortage," *Nursing Administration Quarterly*, Winter 1984.
- "Hospitals Are Us," by Robert Cadamus, M.D., Book Review, *Hospital & Health Services Administration*, Fall 1983.
- "Alternative Scheduling for O.R. Personnel," *Hospitals*, November 16, 1982.

LICENSE
New Jersey Nursing Home Administrators License

EDUCATION
Medical University of South Carolina, DHA, 1999
Washington University, MHA, 1973
University of Connecticut, BA, 1969

MILITARY SERVICE (1969-1971)
First Lieutenant, U.S. Army Medical Service Corps. (Honorable Discharge)

Exhibit 4.2   Resume of Inexperienced Manager

Jane C. Smith
One Any Street • New York, NY 10001 • (212) 000-000 • 111@nyu.edu

EDUCATION:
NEW YORK UNIVERSITY, Robert F. Wagner Graduate School of Public Service, New York, NY
MPA—Health Management and Finance, September 1999, GPA 3.65
Public Service Scholarship Recipient, 1997–1999

UNIVERSITY OF PITTSBURGH, Pittsburgh, PA
BS—Biological Sciences, August 1996, *Cum Laude*
College of Arts and Sciences Study Abroad Scholarship Recipient, Study Abroad Board of Executive
Visitors Meeting guest speaker, Senior Mortar Board Honor Society executive member

EXPERIENCE:
NEW YORK WEILL CORNELL CENTER OF NEW YORK PRESBYTERIAN HOSPITAL,
New York, NY
Administrative Resident, Cornell Physician Organization (PO), 1998–Present
• Benchmarked operations and fiscal management of PO, including billing and collection
  activities for more than $300 million in medical services.
• Participated in implementation of Business Process Redesign of PO billing and collections
  processes with teams from McGladrey & Pullen, LLP and PO Business Office.
• Designed and administered survey of corporate services and marketing strategies of 9
  marketing divisions at PO and New York Presbyterian Hospital. Identified gaps in services to
  develop integrated marketing program.
• Chaired referral management workgroup to review and improve referral process at primary
  care practice of 22 physicians. Designed improvement initiatives and implementation plan to
  streamline and standardize process.
• Analyzed volume trends of PO physician ambulatory services to be presented to the
  Columbia-Cornell Joint Executive Committee. Defined development opportunities in
  selected zip code areas in New York City.
• Organized healthcare management course for 23 PO clinical chairpersons and physician
  leaders in conjunction with NYU Wagner School.
• Developed curriculum for ten-week management course for 32 participating basic science
  and clinical department administrators. Organized and coordinated course with senior
  administration from Medical College, PO, and NYU Wagner School.

NEW YORK CITY DEPARTMENT OF HEALTH, New York, NY
Health Research Training Program (HRTP) Intern, Bureau of Finance, 1997–1998
• Developed implementation plan for decentralized fee-for-services billing program.
• Reviewed requests for proposal regarding patient information system and billing project.
• Recommended sliding fee schedules and centralized process to the Central Billing
  Committee Task Force.

UNIVERSITY OF PITTSBURGH MEDICAL CENTER, Pittsburgh, PA
CPR Instructor, Health Education Office, 1995–1996

CHARING CROSS HOSPITAL & WESTMINSTER MEDICAL SCHOOL, London, England
Physical Therapy Intern, June–Aug 1995

VETERANS AFFAIRS MEDICAL CENTER, Pittsburgh, PA
Physical Therapy Aide, Jan–June 1995

SKILLS:
Emergency Medical Technician (EMT) Certified (1994–1997), CPR Professional Rescuer
Certified (1994–1997), CPR Instructor Certified (1995–1997), and fluency in Mandarin.

EXPERIENCES ABROAD:
Children's Mission Project in Puebla, Mexico (1992) and Overseas Chinese Youth Language
Training and Study Tour in Taipei, Taiwan (1994).

out by the employer to hiring firms). It is not uncommon for advertised jobs in health services management to draw more than 100 inquiries and applicants. As such, strategies aimed at getting an interview as well as getting a job must be well planned and executed. And usually senior managers can have substantial input into ensuring such interviews. Obviously, screeners are going to match up the skills and experience as shown in your resume with the job requirements (which means that just as obviously, you must be able to tailor various resumes to requirements for different positions).

REFERENCE CHECK

You will be asked for references, and you should assume that these references will be checked, usually by telephone. Before listing someone as a reference, ask the person if she is willing to give you a positive recommendation. You should be able to screen out anyone who dislikes you enough to speak poorly of you. But, of course, what you are seeking is an enthusiastic recommendation based on firsthand experience of working with you.

THE INTERVIEW

Try to anticipate questions and be well prepared to answer them. Rehearse answers with family and friends. Remember that you are competing with other well-qualified candidates. Be prepared to show why you can handle certain aspects of the job that are not addressed in your resume. Typical questions interviewers ask include the following:

- Tell me a little about yourself, and about your experience and skills.
- Why do you want this job?
- Name an obstacle in your previous job and how you handled it.
- What are your strengths and weaknesses?
- What kinds of work do you like and not like?
- What kinds of results have you achieved in any phase of your activities?

- What are you looking for in a job?
- What do you plan to be doing in five or ten years?

In answering questions, be direct, brief, clear, and positive. You can build weaknesses into strengths—for example, "I am a perfectionist and am never completely satisfied with my work," or "I am very interested in results, and some people don't like that." There is nothing wrong with answering "I don't know," to questions like "What do you plan to be doing in five or ten years?" Many interviewers lack experience at handling such a response. Therefore, as you prepare, think about how to make sure you get your message across. You may have to carefully redirect the interview.

Be prepared with your own questions for interviewers. "What are the most important aspects of the job?" Show that you have read materials about the organization. "What happened to the previous occupant of the position?" or "Why was this position created now?" To protect yourself, try to find out what risks are involved in the position. Your questions should indicate that you have thought through the requirements of the position and its challenges.

It helps to show enthusiasm about working for a particular organization and a particular management team. Dress like you belong in the job. Listen well. Conduct yourself like a manager. Remember that interviewers are people too, with their own needs and fears. Try to key on some aspect of your skills and experience that the interviewer is looking for. If your skills and experience don't fit with the position, then perhaps the job is not right for you.

JOB SEARCH AS EDUCATION

Job hunting is time consuming and often frustrating, especially when you are seeking employment for the first time. At the same time, a job search can be an excellent opportunity to learn more about yourself, to find out more about how others see you, and to make new contacts. One prospective employer may recommend you to another where they have a job that more closely fits your skills, experience, and preferences. As a result of the search process, you may change what you are looking for in a job because of greater self-knowledge.

SEARCHING FOR YOUR SECOND JOB AND BEYOND

Managers' job options are limited by who they are, where they are willing to go, and what they are willing and prefer to do. Job options are limited by what managers have done up to now, what roles they can perform, what skills and experience they possess, and how well they can communicate and appear to be able to do what they say they can. Generally speaking, the best predictor of future success in a job is a track record of past success in a job that requires similar skills and experience.

How do you know when it's time to move? When you're not learning anything significant and when you have mastered your current job. Don't move unless the new job offer is so much better that it offsets the transfer costs of risk and learning a new political environment. What happens to your career often depends on what happens to your boss, and you should be working on an exit strategy from day one of a new job, just in case the boss changes, dies, or leaves. Certainly if you are finding challenge and opportunity in your current job, and if you are adequately paid—who is ever "overpaid"?—there is certainly nothing wrong with remaining where you are.

Your needs at work change over time, and different managers have different needs and aspirations. While most of us prefer positions of higher status and responsibility, not all of us wish to pay the price of seeking and holding such positions—learning how to perform new roles and to use new skills effectively, changing habits, altering relationships, and assuming more responsibility and risk. It is certainly better to consider changing jobs when you do not have to move rather than when you are forced to do so.

CRITERIA FOR JOB SELECTION

The first decision is whether to actively search for a new position. There are costs involved, not the least of which is the probable loss of trust from your present superiors and colleagues if they find out you are looking. The usual approach here is to wait until you are actively pursuing a job and then to say that the other firm has approached you (even though "I am perfectly happy here"). Obviously time spent searching for a new job is time you cannot spend actively doing your current job.

Once you have decided to start searching again (of course, reading the classifieds in the *New York Times* on Sundays does not mean you are actively searching), principal considerations will include location, travel required, hours of work, type of work and organization, amount of stress, type of boss, culture of the organization, and amount of risk. In considering a job move, it is often easier to rule out what you do not want than to specify what you do want. And the natural place to look, with discretion, for another position is in the organization in which you are already working; who knows you better, and why not?

Location

The advantage of being flexible about where you will work is that you are more likely to find a job you are looking for when you have the whole country (or several countries) to look at. Given the same demand, there is likely to be a greater number of available jobs in geographic areas where health services organizations are expanding than where they are downsizing. Two primary disadvantages of jobs in locations other than where you now live are the cost of search, in terms of finding out what is available when your contacts will be more limited, and uprooting, especially when this involves family members, particularly a spouse who also works.

Travel

Some managerial positions require a great deal of travel. Management consultants, for example, usually spend many nights away from home enduring the vagaries of canceled flights and adjusting to time changes. Some, especially the young and single, find such travel exciting and the changes in assignments challenging.

Hours

Certain jobs, such as that of a hospital administrator, typically require consistently long hours of work. Others, such as planning analyst, may involve intermittent long hours of work. Ambulatory care managers or compliance officers may tend to work regular and shorter hours.

For managers whose chief pleasure in life is meaningful work, positions with long working days may be desirable. For others who wish to spend considerable time with family and kids, shorter workdays and work-weeks will be preferable.

Type of Work and Organization

Some managers prefer to work in only one type of organization, such as a nonprofit hospital or for-profit H M O, or in one type of job, such as line management or planning. Others prefer to work only under one type of auspice—public, nonprofit, or for-profit. Others want a mix of all three or want certain types of positions only at certain phases of their career.

Stress

People vary in their ability to perform effectively and as to their pref-erence or aversion over time for working under stressful conditions. All managers have to adjudicate competing claims on organizational resources and on their time and presence, which tends to be stress-ful. Jobs involving a great deal of stress often pay more and offer higher prestige; they may also provide less job security and may be injurious to your health. The manager's ability to respond effectively under stress is affected by the amount of stress she is accustomed to and her support systems; managers are able to cope better with a great deal of stress at certain periods of their lives rather than at oth-ers. Consider alternating very stressful jobs with less stressful jobs. Recognize that, for many, health services management tends to be stressful in any case.

Boss

Often the most important criterion in evaluating a job is whom you will be working for or reporting to (also important are the persons the manager will be working with and dependent on for effective perfor-mance of her own job). What kind of person does the manager feel most or least comfortable working for? The manager may require or prefer a boss who is highly supportive or at least fair, or someone who will give the manager sufficient discretion to use creativity and judgment, and who will then recognize and reward the manager if performance meets or exceeds mutually agreed-on standards.

It may be difficult to perceive, at least during the recruitment process, what it will be like working for a particular boss in a particular job. Ask others in the organization, preferably peers, what they think. The way the boss treats the manager may change over time, especially as trust is earned. Bosses and managers whose styles and personalities conflict may learn to work acceptably together if each respects what the other has to contribute. Some managers can adjust to different types of superiors, while some superiors can adjust to different kinds of subordinates.

Culture

Given your own culture and the culture you have become used to in working for organizations, is the culture in the organization in which you have been offered a position suitable for you? For example, do managers generally share information with each other, in an informal way, or is hierarchy and going through channels highly emphasized?

How sensitive is the organization to the needs of clients and potential clients in a surrounding community, and how does this sensitivity fit with your own values and preferences? These questions are often not easy for young and inexperienced people to answer, because we all have a tendency to take for granted our present culture and the culture we are used to finding in organizations.

Risk

Risk includes the possibility of not obtaining a desired job and of other people's knowing this, but also, and more importantly, of retaining the new job after it has been obtained. Such risk can be assessed along two dimensions: organizational risk and personal risk. Organizational risks are those over which the manager has no control, such as loss of a major customer or physician group that results in downsizing. Personal risks are those over which managers usually have a degree of control, or at least to which managers have the opportunity to adapt. These risks include such things as political conflicts, instability, the inconsistency and lack of loyalty of a superior, and the manager's own lack of skills and experience.

Reasons for seeking a high-risk job usually relate to the opportunity for greater reward. In actuality a manager's risk may be lower than generally perceived because the manager knows that, unlike many others, she has the skills and experience to do the job effectively. In changing jobs, managers may be trading the comfort of a present position for one with greater responsibilities and rewards but also greater risks.

Selecting Among Alternative Job Opportunities

Managers often have to choose among competing job options, especially when starting out, and the choice can often feel like choosing between apples and oranges. A useful approach is to use decision criteria, as planners do. But be mindful that criteria are often used to rationalize a choice rather than make one; if a particular option is preferred, for whatever reason, the selector is free to change the criteria.

First, evaluate your current position in terms of what you like about it, don't like about it, or are indifferent to. Second, specify a set of job criteria along the lines of the factors we have been discussing—location, boss, and risk. Third, list or numerically score each factor and calculate a total score. These steps will not necessarily make the choice simple, but they should assist you in specifying all elements necessary in such a choice and in clarifying the reasons that underlie your preferences.

A GOOD FIT

Managerial effectiveness, and therefore job satisfaction, may be primarily about the relationships between a manager and a job, and between a manager and coworkers, rather than about the abilities of the manager. That is, although job satisfaction is highly determined by the manager's expectations, the same manager may be very effective in one position and not effective in another. If this is so, managers in a job search or in the pursuit of excellence need to spend more time reflecting on and evaluating the fit between their skills and experience and the job requirements. One good way to do this is to understand the success of the previous job occupant, examine how his skills and experience resemble your own, and estimate whether the job is still the same or whether it has changed. Understanding your own successes and how to build on them is also critical. Making calculations as to good fit assumes good self-knowledge, which many managers lack. Therefore, whatever you think of yourself, your skills, experience, and preferences, compare your thoughts with those of your peers and friends.

EXIT STRATEGY

Hospital managers often stress the importance of discharge planning on the day the patient is admitted to the hospital. What many managers do not pay sufficient attention to in managing their careers is the importance of a good exit strategy in taking any job—figuring out in advance how to know whether the job is not working out, and, if that is the case, planning what to do next.

IMPROVING YOUR PRESENT SITUATION

An alternative to seeking a new job (and consistent with such a search) is increasing the benefits the manager derives from his present position, decreasing the costs, or both. Some may be content as they are; continuous improvement is not always a priority. Moreover, benefits and costs are perceived differently by different managers. Manager A wants more money and Manager B wants more responsibility; or Manager C wants an assistant while Manager D wants to shuck certain functional responsibilities.

Example: *Lou Baines has been working as assistant administrator at Highsmith Hospital, a 750-bed urban teaching institution, for three years. Baines feels that he is ready for a new job, but he likes working at Highsmith. His superior, Nora Wainwright, the associate administrator,* cautions Baines to wait, assuring him that he is appreciated. Baines feels, however, that Wainwright's star is waning with Cal Calderone, M.D., chief executive officer. How can Baines improve his present position at Highsmith? Will approaching Calderone injure his present relationship with Wainwright? Can approaching Calderone hurt his prospects of finding a better job?

Baines can do nothing, can seek another position outside of Highsmith, or can discuss the situation with Calderone. A fourth option, which many less experienced managers may ignore, is for Baines to discuss with Wainwright ways of improving his present situation. If Baines feels that he is being fairly paid for his present responsibility, he can ask Wainwright for more responsibility. If Baines feels that he is being underpaid, he can ask for more money, or for more money as well as greater responsibility. Baines should be prepared to respond to questions following from his proposal. Will Wainwright, or someone else, agree to the transfer of responsibilities? Does Wainwright feel that Baines has been doing well enough with his current responsibilities? It may be important for Baines to gain Wainwright's approval of suggested action before discussing it with Calderone. Calderone is certain to ask Baines what Wainwright thinks and then to discuss it with Wainwright.

CHANGING ASPIRATIONS OR PERFORMANCE

To improve the situation, a manager can either change his circumstances or change his attitude about present circumstances. These two approaches tend to be mutually exclusive. Those who seek promotion or new employment tend to seek more and new responsibilities, while those who seek more satisfaction tend to want to do what they have been doing with the least required effort. There are, of course, exceptions to these tendencies. An aspiring manager may spend more time pursuing advancement than contributing through hard work to organizational effectiveness. A satisfied manager may yet seek more and new responsibilities because he has been successful and wants to contribute more without spending a great deal of time planning for promotion, higher remuneration, or a job somewhere else.

Asking for More

If the manager does not ask, he will not receive. The boss may not be aware of managerial preferences. The boss may not want the manager to ask for more money or less responsibility—and that may be why the manager hasn't asked. If the manager asks for more work, the boss may raise questions about current performance.

What the manager wants to consider carefully, however, is asking for something for which the asking or the thing itself involves high risk. If the manager asks for something that will not please him if granted, the manager loses credibility. The manager may want more responsibility for more areas or functions because it gives him higher status and makes him feel that he is a higher performer than he really is or than he is relative to other managers. The manager may think he can be responsible for the additional area or function because he does not have a clear idea of what it takes to get that set of tasks done properly. The manager may be comparing what he can do with what an ineffective manager is currently doing, without sufficiently considering why the current manager has become ineffective or what is really causing the problem.

Rationales for asking for "more" include the following: when the pay offered for a new job is less than what the manager has previously earned, when pay is out of line relative to other managers in the organization or to comparable managers in other organizations, or when a raise may have an effect on present and future productivity. However, unless the original terms of employment were decidedly unfair or managerial performance or the job has changed significantly, why should the boss authorize a raise, other than what everyone else gets, assuming that the boss has the authority to do so? It is possible, although unlikely, that the boss will give the manager a raise as a morale-booster. A more likely situation would occur when another manager leaves and the remaining manager is asked to take over additional responsibilities while continuing to be responsible for previous responsibilities at a slightly higher salary.

As bonus plans become more common, pay negotiations will likely be carried on regarding the basis for bonuses and whether targets were achieved.

When a manager asks for a raise, or that his bonus be calculated in a manner different than planned, the boss must consider the alternative of not granting the manager's request. Will the manager agree with the boss's rating of current managerial performance? What problems will granting the manager's request create for the boss with other members of the top management team? Will the boss have to give others more too, or change the way their bonuses are calculated? Other typical arguments to justify a denial include "we can't afford it," "I'll see what I can do about it next year," and "I'm for it, but my boss won't let me give it to you."

If the manager feels she is being treated unfairly, she should not threaten the boss unless she is willing to carry out the threat. If the manager wishes to inflict damage, this is accomplished not by threatening, but by carrying out whatever it is that she intended to do. If the manager threatens to leave, the boss may ask for her resignation. It is better to leave on good terms with the boss, especially if the manager has decided to leave but has no job offer in hand. The boss may give the manager bad references, make the manager's present job more miserable, or give the manager less money or benefits on leaving than what the manager thinks she is entitled to. For example, the boss may have counted vacation days differently for the past four years, and the manager may have nothing in writing to justify the number of days she thinks she is entitled to.

The best way to get paid what the manager feels he deserves is to secure advantageous terms before accepting a position, when the manager's bargaining position is generally strongest. Once employed, switching jobs costs the manager more, in noneconomic terms. These costs decrease, of course, once a new job offer is in hand. It is also easier for the boss to pay the manager more initially because she can explain to others on the management team why the increased pay was necessary to recruit the manager into the organization.

Asking for Less

There are several compelling arguments for asking for "less": the manager will be able to perform his other responsibilities better, the manager is willing to take less pay, or the work in question can be left undone with little harm to the organization. The manager may want to do less for reasons of health or other interests or because the manager wants to focus effort and work more effectively in specific areas. If the manager feels that he is working too hard and wants less responsibility, it always helps to find someone else who wants to do whatever it is that he does not want to do.

The boss may be delighted to learn that a manager is willing to do more or to do less, because it fits in with the boss's own plans. The boss may have been afraid that additional work would make the manager feel overburdened relative to peer managers, or he may have feared that the manager would resent being relieved of responsibilities that, for whatever reason, the boss believes another member of the team can more effectively carry out.

On the other hand, rather than decrease the manager's responsibilities, the boss may prefer to replace the manager with someone else who would contribute more and be paid less to do what the manager is doing. If the manager has contributed a great deal to the organization for many years, the boss may be constrained not to get rid of him. It is certainly partly the organization's fault if a manager fails to contribute after having been employed for several years. If the situation cannot be remedied, the manager should be assisted, financially and otherwise, in finding other employment or in accepting early retirement. However, managers cannot count on receiving such assistance.

Managing Yourself

"Our judgment is in great part what other people think it is."

—Ray Brown, *Judgment in Administration,* 1966

WHEN WORKING WITH OTHERS, YOU HAVE most control over yourself. You control your own behavior and, to an extent, how you use your time and where you put your physical presence. Much time can be wasted attempting to manage things that cannot be controlled. In this chapter, we examine four managerial competencies—keeping informed, earning trust, understanding values, and making decisions—and use examples to stimulate thinking. Next, we discuss how a manager can choose to manage her time and presence to attain organizational and personal goals. We then examine considerations in behaving ethically as a manager. We conclude by focusing on how to manage oneself in relationship with others, and most particularly with the boss.

KEEPING INFORMED

Example: *Claire Rogers, Director of Clinical Services at Highsmith Teaching Hospital, seeks to improve nursing department productivity, yet she has no clear-cut way of measuring nursing contribution to health outcomes or even to length of stay. The* CEO *wants to reduce nursing costs consistent with maintaining acceptable quality.*

Rogers is expected to know the best practices in nursing operations and the performance of the hospital's competitors. Information is available as to typical and Highsmith Hospital staffing patterns by service and patient mix and regarding standard measures of quality of care, ranging from nosocomial infections to adverse drug reactions. Rogers is expected to know the current problems and concerns of the hospital nursing staff and the desired levels of performance. She should also have a plan to get the nursing staff from where it is to where she and the nurses want it to be. Rogers is expected as well to be able to document her conclusions, including the quality of care.

Managers have greater access to and control of certain information by virtue of their position. For example, hospital managers regularly receive information about governmental regulations and compliance advice. Much internal communication must go through a manager's office before it is sent throughout the organization. Healthcare, like other sectors, is becoming more cost-sensitive. Managers often have to approve resource requests for items ranging from new personnel slots to the allocation of space to new equipment. Therefore, anyone who wants organizational resources generally seeks support or tolerance from managers before making a serious formal claim.

In an ideal world, managers have sufficient time and staff assistance to learn how other organizations respond to challenges and develop the data needed for decision making. Managers want to know such things as what services similar organizations are expanding or closing out, industry standards for cost per unit of service, collection rates, average days in accounts payable, payment rates, how other organizations recruit physicians and key employees, and how they respond to patient complaints. The list is long, and managers can and do acquire more information than they can process effectively.

Managers must structure what they need to know to meet performance requirements. How is the manager evaluated and by whom? What kinds of data do evaluators need for such evaluations? What data will convince evaluators that the manager is making an essential contribution? Managers also require information about the organization's political situations, including who the allies and opponents are and how to find and use such information to take appropriate actions?

A common error of entry-level managers is to define as "unimportant" what members of the organization's controlling coalition define differently. This is related to a manager's not knowing who is "important" where she works. Of course, everyone is important, but some are more important than others. A second error is spending too much attention on problems and issues that the organization or unit cannot solve or is not ready to solve. There is often a cost involved in getting useful information. Remember that managers must act based on limited information. If you are uncomfortable with this, consider alternative career opportunities.

EARNING TRUST

Example: *Stan Lewis, Urban* HMO *Marketing Director, meets regularly with Gloria Lopez, President of the* HMO*'s community advisory board. Lopez complains about discrimination against Hispanic workers and patients and wants the community board to have the final say about* HMO *budget decisions. Lewis explains that the board is advisory, that any complaint she makes will be looked into and results explained. The community advisory board can discuss all budget items, but final decisions will be made by* HMO *management.*

Here is a situation in which some interests conflict. Lopez, a former worker in the HMO, seeks jobs and dignity for Hispanic workers, some of whom are her friends. Lewis may not earn her trust, but he can convince her that he is trustworthy. From his point of view, some of her complaints may be justified. They may disagree, but over time they may come to respect the hard work and competence each brings to the bargaining table.

If a large part of managerial success or avoidance of failure depends on obtaining the trust of others, how are you going to earn and build this trust? Gaining trust is easier than having to regain it after it has been lost. Trust is earned over time, as others observe your consistency, monitor your decisions, and judge whether you are taking their values into account as you make and implement decisions.

The manager's age and experience affect how she is perceived and trusted in an organization. People are generally less willing to trust a young and inexperienced manager, often with good reason, which is why such managers should listen and "blend in" until getting established through job performance and, therefore, earned trust.

UNDERSTANDING VALUES

Example: *Wyatt Burns, Planning Vice President for Urban* HMO, *does not understand why two of his subordinates have been promoted to regional presidencies of sub-unit* HMOs *by Grand Alliance* HMO, *a national plan with four million members. Burns has been with Urban* HMO *for 20 years and is acknowledged as brainy, energetic, and productive. Tim MacGregor, President and* CEO *of Grand Alliance, tells Burns that he was not offered one of the sub-unit* HMO *presidencies because of his lack of line experience. The other three individuals are white; Burns is an African-American. One of those promoted tells Burns subsequently that he thinks MacGregor feels that Burns is unpredictable in his loyalty to the organization and does not feel as safe with Burns as with the other managers.*

Being a minority group manager is definitely different. However unfair, perceptions of minority managers are often stereotyped, and managers from minority groups may have to be more convincing in their performance to shift those perceptions. Joe Burgess, former assistant vice president for New York City Health and Hospitals Corporation, suggests identifying that there is a problem, recognizing that you cannot change the organization overnight, and going where what you have to offer is better accepted and appreciated.[22]

There is often no right or wrong when values clash. There is behavior that works or does not work over the short-term or long-term in the perception of managers who are themselves changing in composition and in intensity of feelings. Know your own values and how they differ from your superiors or subordinates before you act. This is so for physician managers as well as for African-American or female managers. Obviously managers should consider differences in values before accepting a position. If you have strong feelings against profits in healthcare or if you dislike participative management, do not work for those organizations or those managers. Of course, you can always fight to change other people's behavior, if you are willing to pay the price. The authors' judgment is that in making the calculation, most managers would not be so willing.

MAKING DECISIONS

Example: *Lisle Kent, President of Deaconess Medical Center, has been advised by the new chief financial officer, Victor Alan, that the hospital will lose $7 million next year on $200 million sales unless remedial action is taken. Kent has been informed by Hazel Consultants that the medical center has 4.5 full-time equivalent (FTE) employees per average daily census, as compared with 4.0, the standard for similar hospitals. Hazel will charge the hospital $1 million to "fix the problem." Board members wonder why Kent hasn't been "on top" of the situation. Should Alan recommend hiring Hazel consultants? Should Kent consider salary cuts for top management?*

Managers may judge problems to be more serious than they are, may recommend unnecessary action and generate unnecessary conflict, or may underrate the importance of serious problems and fail to respond quickly enough. In the above example, Kent has defined the problem as serious enough and beyond the competence of current management to resolve in the short run. He must now consider appropriate action so his behavior is viewed as appropriate by other stakeholders—that is, board members and employees.

Health services managers do not spend most of their time making organizational decisions. Unlike the decision that Kent faces regarding the consultants, the decisions most managers make are more often what to say to whom and how to say it. The basic resource at your disposal is yourself—that is, who you are and what you say. Therefore, think before you speak, keep yourself informed, work on understanding how others view situations, and do your homework before speaking out.

MANAGING TIME AND PRESENCE

The number of hours managers work on the job varies. Who is to say that the person who works twice as many hours contributes twice as much, or even any more, to organizational effectiveness? On the other hand, it is hard to argue that a manager working so many more hours will not accomplish or contribute more.

Most managers spend long hours working at home, especially doing paperwork. There may be fewer interruptions at home, and therefore more can be accomplished in a given period of time. Others make work-related phone calls after hours for the same reasons. Ross Webber has suggested the following tactics for managing your time:

- Insulate yourself from incoming communications.
- Isolate yourself or withdraw physically, so interruptions are eliminated, except in emergencies.
- Set aside a time to respond to messages all at once, and consider delegating some to others in the organization.

Webber cautions that the manager should not minimize available time for response, which he feels should make up more than half the manager's time. Moreover, he recommends that managers "be open, patient and truly responsive" during response time.[23]

How should time at work be allocated? Much of this choice is made for the manager by others. But analyze how you spend your time for a typical two-week period, then decide which kinds of activities you want or need to spend more or less time on. Don't forget to schedule some uninterrupted blocks of the time during the week or month for important planning and other creative work. Many managers get so caught up in work that they forego time in reflection and thinking about what is happening around them and thus are unable to respond appropriately.

Managing your presence can be important. Others may feel more comfortable talking with you in their own work areas, where you may sample their work performance. Off-the-job presence can also be important. Opportunities for interaction with staff and with customers can occur at the supermarket, the gym, in the physician's office, or attending PTA meetings. There are no set rules for how much time you should spend in different locations. Visiting with others and responding to their concerns takes time. But it is important to reflect on where and with whom you are spending time, if you are to effectively manage it.

BEHAVING ETHICALLY

Example: *Sam Stith, Glory Hospital lab technician, informs* CEO *Victor Alan that Sally Bruin,* PH.D., *laboratory department head, is not sending out certain infrequently performed lab tests, but reports back to physicians that results are normal. When Alan asks Bruin about this, she insists that all tests are sent out and asks why Alan would think otherwise.*

Obviously, Alan has questions of fact regarding Bruin's behavior. But he also must decide whether and what kind of further investigation is necessary. What is his responsibility to patients, physicians, Stith, and Bruin? These are not so much questions of right and wrong as of ethical responsibility and understanding the benefits and risks of making "ethical" decisions.

The benefit of a professional ethical code is that it encourages you to take the larger view of your job and responsibility as a manager. It doesn't necessarily tell you what to do in a specific situation. In our experience, we have found that integrity pays. As to what "integrity" means, think in terms of behavioral consistency and how you would feel if what you know behind closed doors was accurately reported in the local media. In the long run, communities or customers will reward organizations that act responsibly. Superiors will reward managers who behave with integrity. Such organizations and managers are trusted and rewarded because stakeholders know that the person or organization can be counted on to do the right thing at the right time. Not only must you behave in an ethical way but you must be seen as behaving so.

MANAGING YOUR RELATIONSHIP WITH OTHERS

Example: *Lisle Kent, Deaconess Medical Center* CEO, *has been asked by board member Luther Rawlins to develop a governance management information system so that the board can properly carry out evaluation*

*of managerial and organizational performance and long-range plan-
ning. Currently, the board gets extensive financial information on performance relative to budget for the ten operating units of the medical
center, but no regular information on market share by product line, updating or revising of the current strategic plan, or physician and customer perceptions of service. The board chair, Delbert Diggs, is relatively
indifferent to Rawlins' proposal.*

How do managers such as Kent respond to the demands of persons
such as Rawlins who have limited individual authority over them?
Peter Block (1987) has divided people into four categories on any issue based on agreement and trust. Where there is high trust and high
agreement, persons are *allies* with whom managers affirm agreement
on a project or vision, reaffirm the quality of the relationship and ask
for advice and support. Where there is low agreement and low trust,
persons are *adversaries,* and Block recommends that managers state
their vision for a project, state in a neutral way their understanding of
an adversary's position, identify their own contribution to the problem, and end the meeting with plans and no demand.

Assuming in the case of Kent and Rawlins that there is high trust
and low agreement, Block would categorize them as *opponents,* for
whom Block suggests managers should be grateful, as they can bring
the picture of reality and practicality to our plans. With opponents,
Block suggests that managers engage in problem-solving. Kent could
respond by saying something like "How does this relate to our goals
and strategy?" or "I agree with you, let's look at some critical human
resource issues" or "I'll try to get information on best practices in this
area in other organizations and report back."[24] Where there is high
agreement and low trust, persons are *bedfellows.* Block recommends
reaffirming the agreement and acknowledging that caution exists. Be
clear about what each wants from the other and try to reach some
agreement on how to work together.

MANAGING THE RELATIONSHIP WITH YOUR BOSS

Example: *Dagmar Neustadt, Vice President of Patient Services at Metro
Hospital, has worked for two years to improve the level of customer service
for patients and physicians. This week the management staff completed*

the initial budget planning for the upcoming fiscal year. The proposed budget calls for an $800,000 reduction in expenses, and Neustadt's division has to absorb 40 percent of it. In exploring the alternative cost-reduction plans, Neustadt has committed to maintaining the patient-staff interface. With that goal, her options are limited and point to eliminating a level of management that currently reports to her. She has built this staff into a loyal, hard-working, focused team.

What is Neustadt's obligation to those who have been loyal to her and to the organization? How does an organization deal with restructuring and downsizing and still expect its managers to perform at high levels? Does the concept of loyalty work in two directions?

What the Boss Expects

The boss wants loyalty. Loyal managers think about how some action or decision will affect the boss and the boss's position personally. Loyal managers tell the boss in advance and at an appropriate time and place when they think the boss is wrong and back the boss wholeheartedly after the decision has been made no matter which way it goes.

The boss expects you to do what you said you will do unless circumstances dictate a change in plan. An important change should be cleared in advance. The boss expects a certain level of managerial value added, expressed in terms of changes in performance in the departments or units you supervise. The boss wants to know how to help you accomplish the goals you have said you will accomplish. The boss wants no surprises. Tell him the bad news accurately and sufficiently in advance so he can respond adequately and calmly.

The boss would like you to be cheerful and take yourself seriously, but not too seriously. The boss has enough problems without worrying about your mental health. The boss's position demands respect and courtesy, which is the least you can give the person who decides whether you keep your position, what your working conditions are, and how much you are paid. The boss expects political savvy. You don't tell others you are implementing a decision because the boss said so; you give them the reasons behind the decision. If you can't think of some good and sufficient reasons, ask why they are having difficulties with the decision or its implementation and tell them you will discuss their views with the boss.

What the Manager Expects

You expect the boss to explain what the important job requirements are and how and when work must be completed. Put this in writing to avoid misunderstanding. You expect to be given sufficient autonomy to do what is expected. You should not have to check back for approval of every action. As a new manager, you should expect close supervision at first. You expect to be rewarded adequately and fairly relative to your peers.

All workers should expect to be evaluated. You can be fired after receiving excellent evaluations, but that is not the point. You can't be expected to change your behavior unless the boss explains what he expects you to do or stop doing and how. You won't be as helpful to the boss as you could be unless he explains how your work fits into his plan and his plan into the overall organizational strategy. It is reasonable for you to ask for an evaluation. If it is not forthcoming, suggest that you would like to do a self-evaluation and have the boss critique it.

As the boss expects your loyalty to him or her, you expect the boss to protect you. Expect some consideration as an individual as well. Before asking you to undertake a challenging assignment, the boss should ask your opinion and feelings so that both of you can consider whether and how best you can do what he asks and how he asks it.

Why the Boss Does Not Get from You What He Wants

If your performance does not meet minimum requirements, the boss will try to get rid of you, or you will look for work elsewhere. Expectations may not have been clear, or they may been misinterpreted. Perhaps what you were asked to do was unrealistic to begin with but neither of you realized it at the outset. You may be afraid to renegotiate what had been agreed to, expecting that the boss will not see things as you do. Why didn't you tell him in advance about constraints to your making the expected contribution, about conflicting demands that prevented you from meeting deadlines? The boss may see you as lacking certain skills or experience because of inconsistencies in his expectations. You may be afraid to ask the boss for help because it would make you look stupid or because you don't want to appear dependent on others.

It may take too much time for the boss to supervise you effectively. Perhaps you feel smarter or better educated than your boss. Perhaps you don't like each other as individuals. Perhaps you want to blame the boss for your own mistakes. Sometimes events happen so fast that you don't have time to warn the boss. The bad news may be inaccurate, and you may lack the time or skills to validate it before telling him. Perhaps the physicians in the organization want to get rid of your boss; if you stand up and defend him they will want to get rid of you too.

Cheerfulness, a sense of humor, and respect are hard to manufacture. Certain bosses may not like excessive cheerfulness, humor, or deference. Most managers are not born with political savvy and do not learn it at school; even if you acquire such savvy, you are likely to continue to make errors of judgment and approach under stress and in the face of conflicting pressures.

Why You Don't Get from the Boss What You Want

When circumstances change, what the boss told you earlier may no longer apply. You may not be rewarded adequately because your bargaining power is weak and the boss has a fixed amount of money or status to dispense. His main concern may be to protect his own job rather than attain organizational goals and implement organizational strategy. The boss may not want to tell you that you are doing well for fear that you will slack off or become overconfident. The boss may not see "empowerment" as in his own interest.

The boss may not explain how what you do fits into the big picture because he wants to limit your power by denying you information. Perhaps he wants you to deflect antagonism away from him and toward yourself. Filling you in takes time, and he may lack the time or find your needs a low priority. The boss may not reward you relative to your performance because he places a different value on your contribution than you do. He may not have picked you or may not like you, and he may think you should be working harder, more effectively, or more loyally.

So Where Is Justice?

In sum, there may be good reasons why you and your boss (or you and your subordinates) don't agree, both on organizational and on personal matters. Frequent and frank communication is essential to minimize differences of expectation and to adequately explore finer points in implementation of organizational strategy and on human resources development. Such communication will not take place without some conflict. It may be uncomfortable, but it is unavoidable.

Do not expect justice in organizational life. If you expect the ideal, you may be denied the acceptable. If, however, you are making significant contributions to your organization and others see that you are, it is likely that you will be asked to continue to make them, if not in the current organization, then in another one. If your expectations for rewards are too high relative to your boss's, they are likely to be lowered over time as you become aware of others' perceptions. Or perhaps you can raise the level of your performance. If your expectations are too low relative to the boss's, perhaps you are being taken advantage of or will be unexpectedly rewarded.

6
Managing Your Team

The essential strategy of leadership in mobilizing power is to recognize the arrays of motives and goals in potential followers, to appeal to those motives by words and action, and to strengthen those motives and goals in order to increase the power of leadership, thereby changing the environment with which both followers and leaders act.

— James MacGregor Burns, *Leadership,* 1978

MANAGERS DO NOT WORK BY THEMSELVES BUT as part of a management team. This team includes other managers, support staff at work, and personal support at home. This chapter is divided into the following parts: managerial support, peers and subordinates, working on a new management team, recruiting and retaining managers, keeping a team motivated, management reorganization, working with temporary allies, and managing a family.

Managers face conflicting pressures. On the one hand, they may want to reveal themselves and be loved for who they are. On the other hand, they may not wish to mix their managerial and private lives. They may view their private natures as more important than, and necessarily separate from, their managerial roles. Managers may learn over time how to effectively separate their managerial roles from their private selves or how to combine the two in ways that best fit their circumstances.

The manager confronts conflicting pressures in dealing with team members or managerial teams. The manager has his own team, and he is part of his superior's team; the manager is also on the management teams of other managers, at least for certain projects. Should managers treat team members primarily as important cogs in an organizational machine, or should he first respond to them as people, and only secondarily as workers? Should the manager's first loyalty be to the team worker or to the organization, and does the manager have to choose?

As with many value questions, there are no right or wrong answers to these questions, only trade-offs. Managers may be able to generalize their actions and attitudes toward others and yet consistently make appropriate exceptions to any generalizations. Such behavior may be instinctive. In the face of conflicting values, managers may not wish to be always reasoning out their behavior. Managerial explanations for behavior are often rationalizations created after the fact rather than by logical and sequential weighting of pros and cons beforehand.

Example: *Manager Sam Martinez hires Harry Fong, fires Claire Bechet, and promotes Lillian Harding not as a scientific exercise in human resources management, but because he feels that Fong can do the job, Bechet has been given a fair chance, and Harding has earned her promotion.*

Martinez's actions are a signal to others that they, too, will be rewarded for effective contribution to the organization. Martinez can deny Fong the data system he needs even though there is good logic to Fong's request. Firing Bechet does not mean that Martinez dislikes her or that Martinez will not assist Bechet in obtaining a job somewhere else, just as promoting Harding does not mean that Martinez necessarily likes her.

If the manager tries to do everything himself, he limits his potential to accomplish goals through others. The non-delegator is unlikely to satisfy the aspirations and expectations of highly educated and aspiring team workers. A leader must know when to act, delegate, or do nothing; be able to see which goals involve the wants and needs of followers; and be capable of acting in the face of rapidly changing and often ambiguous circumstances.

MANAGERIAL SUPPORT

At one time, the entry-level manager either had immediate access to a secretary or shortly gained this privilege. In today's work environment, the manager's support staff is likely to include more machines than human beings—voice mail, e-mail, word processing, and the Internet.

Secretaries, who are often called administrative (or executive) assistants, and receptionists have their own goals and aspirations. An effective secretary can greatly improve managerial contribution. She is another set of "managerial ears," which can be invaluable in understanding organizational politics. She manages access to the manager. Secretaries can protect managerial time by shielding the manager from people to whom others can respond satisfactorily, or they can facilitate access to the senior manager when appropriate. Secretarial work is usually expected to be longer term or at least unconditionally termed, although many secretaries have gone on to managerial positions. Managers should establish a good relationship with their superiors' secretaries, as they may be able to facilitate access for the manager.

What managers expect from administrative assistants and administrative residents or "assistants-to" is long hours and hard work, persistence in getting the details right, accuracy in reporting, a gift for avoiding political controversy, and the ability to listen and to be seen by others as listening to what they are saying. Senior managers expect assistants-to will get their major gratification from work rather than from leisure activities, and that, after orientation, they will be able to perform, usually with help, managerial tasks (to include operating support equipment) such as evaluating compliance with governmental regulations or analyzing budget variance.

Assistants-to should expect their superiors to tell them what is expected at work, to reveal underlying assumptions in making and implementing decisions so that they can learn, and to assist with career development. They can expect managers to set a standard for quality and quantity of contribution, evaluate their performance, and help improve it. They should expect as well consideration and respect as individuals. Most assistants-to jobs are viewed as temporary both by the manager and the assistant-to, so frank discussion of next steps should be undertaken prior to hiring and regularly thereafter. A successful subordinate/superior relationship is a mutual commitment, characterized by mutual adjustment of both parties.

PEERS AND SUBORDINATES

Managerial peers and subordinates can be divided into line and staff. Line managers run separate departments and report to a manager who may be responsible for several departments. Staff managers provide support services to line managers (some staff managers see their job as containing and controlling line managers rather than giving them support). Line and staff managers may have reporting relationships to supervising managers indicated on organizational charts as a straight line or a dotted line (advisory). But line and staff managers commonly have allegiance and loyalty to persons and organizations other than the supervising manager and the organization. For example, the department head for inhalation therapy has an allegiance to pulmonary physicians for clinical matters, or to the professional organization of inhalation therapists for productivity standards.

It is often difficult for newer managers to gain and keep the respect of senior department heads and unit directors of staff services such as finance and information systems. Such department heads and unit directors often know more about their work than and have much greater seniority in the organization than does the new manager.

Managers, and young managers in particular, have to work hard to foster a spirit of teamwork. Although team members may be expected to differ on certain issues because of their different constituencies, they should be able to work together on a broad range of issues, before and after decisions have been reached. They are members of the same organization and have common interests, such as obtaining revenues and gaining market share. Can team workers remain trusting of each other despite occasional conflicting interests? Not always or completely, but a climate of trust is something valuable and well worth working hard to develop and maintain. When trust permeates an organization, greater attention can be paid to job accomplishment and the obtaining of additional resources. There is less bickering and with-drawal of effort and energy from the work itself. The importance of developing a climate of trust among managerial team members, usu-ally as related to the organization's mission and to the vision and be-havior of top management, in part may explain the commitment of certain larger organizations to generally promote from within, ensur-ing career development within the system and creating a sense of "fam-ily" among the management team.

WORKING ON A NEW TEAM

The hiring of a manager will affect everyone who works with her, particularly those who think that they should have gotten her job. In addition, other workers may feel that the new manager's remunera-tion is out of line with their own. Be aware of such feelings on the part of others whom you consider part of your managerial team.

Starting a new job is always difficult, especially if job requirements differ significantly from those of the manager's last job or if it is her first job. The boss should make an extra effort during the first few months on the job to make the new manager feel at home and to help overcome problems in adjusting to a new environment. Such prob-lems are compounded when the manager and her family have made a geographical move.

When starting a new job, remember that somebody else's manage-ment team is already in place. Existing department heads and unit directors may worry and be uncertain. Some may think they will benefit from the manager's joining the organization; others may not. The man-ager has been recruited often to implement policies that are at vari-ance with those of a predecessor. New priorities or approaches will fit better with the skills, experience, and preferences of certain depart-ment heads and unit directors, but not with others.

A new manager enters a politically uncertain job environment and must trust those on whom she depends. When a new manager takes over as chief executive for an entire organization, the wonder is not that so many department heads and administrative staff resign or are fired, but that so many choose or are chosen to stay on. The reasons are varied and relate to the job options and past job satisfaction of incumbents. There are only so many tasks that the new CEO can do at any one time, and effective recruitment of managerial personnel is often a lengthy and problematic process. The new CEO may see most department heads and administrative staff as technically proficient and politically harmless.

The history of the organization may determine how incumbents behave. Was the prior manager in place only for a short period of time, with rapid turnover? Was the prior manager interventionist or laissez-faire? Depending on recent history, the incumbents may be eager to demonstrate loyalty to the new boss, or they may hold back. It may still be a reasonable step to begin to change staff. An organization without any turnover may become stagnant. Realistic turnover can be useful in changing the culture or the way an organization works.

For subordinates to readjust their thinking and performance for a new CEO is not easy—especially when the new chief executive's personality and view of the job contrast sharply with those of a predecessor. It may be difficult to respond to the push of a new CEO who may not be long for the job (or to the pull of old managers who may be on their way out). At such times of change, the subordinate should not pursue new, independent managerial initiatives. Rather, the subordinate manager should concentrate on support activities—and the demand for this kind of contribution is usually greater than the manager can effectively supply.

RECRUITMENT AND RETENTION

Many health services organizations do a poor job of recruiting and retaining vital managerial resources. They do not devote enough resources to the effort and are not sufficiently organized. Nor is the recruitment and retention effort subject to sufficient planning and evaluation. Contrast the effort that goes into selecting and maintaining a $400,000 piece of equipment with a useful life of ten years to the effort that goes into selecting and evaluating an entry-level manager who earns $40,000 a year and who can work for the organization for 30 years and be more productive as well.

Effective recruitment of a managerial team (and of all employees) can enhance the reputation of a health services organization. There may be political repercussions when certain job applicants are rejected. Every job applicant is a potential patient or relative of somebody important to the organization. Often an organization will not be able to recruit its first choice among candidates because of money, location, another job offer, or other reasons. Thus, it is important to show courtesy to all candidates. The person doing the recruitment should respond promptly to all candidates and tell them whether they are being seriously considered, what the nature of the recruiting process is, and when they can expect to learn the outcome.

Recruiting from within has advantages and disadvantages. The promotion of certain individuals with excellent technical backgrounds is risky unless they are supported developmentally with regard to new managerial responsibilities. The skills, experience, and beliefs necessary to excel at being a technician or department head are often not the same as those required to excel as a manager. Doing a job well is different from motivating others to do a job well. Once a promotion is given to a loyal, hardworking subordinate, it is difficult to demote him. If a technician is promoted to department head and then does not perform well, the organization may have lost a good technician and gained a poor department head.

Knowing the organization well is both an advantage and a disadvantage for new managers. They may accept, uncritically, current structure and function. Others in the organization may persist in viewing them in terms of their past positions and responsibilities. The organization may not expect as much from an inside appointee as it would from someone outside. Newly promoted managers may be vulnerable if they lack the formal qualifications usually required for such positions, such as a master's degree in health services management. Furthermore, their judgment may be open to question; if they lack such formal qualifications, they may make some otherwise understandable mistakes and errors soon after they are appointed. Internal candidates may explore their own training needs with their new boss. Again, training agreements are easier to negotiate at the beginning.

KEEPING YOUR TEAM MOTIVATED

There are no simple ways of keeping your managerial team motivated, or, for that matter, of keeping yourself motivated. The aphorism, "if it ain't broke, don't fix it," applies here. If individuals are performing well, don't interfere with them.

Some people do not need to be motivated by anyone else. These self-starters will, if adequately informed and supported, work with energy and grace to accomplish mutually agreed-on goals. In addition, they may make helpful suggestions for changes in response to changing circumstances and may give those to whom they report needed feedback on aspects of managerial performance.

On the other hand, there are individuals who will not or cannot change their performance. If the organization is large enough, there may be other positions in which such people can perform adequately. If not, their services have to be terminated (some manager must fire them). This is never a pleasant process. An organization is not a democracy. Organizations obtain resources for limited purposes rather than as ends in themselves. If ineffective people are permitted to continue to draw paychecks, their work must be done by others, done ineffectively, or not done at all. Presumably, in the last analysis, the patient or the client suffers.

Managers must focus their energies on motivating those individuals (and teams) who, with help, can perform effectively. Individuals can be categorized (validly or invalidly) into categories, such as "works well without close supervision," "works well with close supervision," and "cannot work sufficiently well, even with close supervision." The same individuals may fall into different categories at different times or in regard to different aspects of their work. Categorizing accurately may be problematic; excellent subordinates and support staff can make ineffective managers or department heads look good for a while, and effective managers or department heads may be temporarily incapacitated by a death in the family, illness, or other personal reason.

When the manager is dissatisfied with a team member's performance, ask if the dissatisfaction is with the results of the subordinate's performance or with his style? Put another way, is this problem a matter of the team member's lack of knowledge, poor judgment, or bad attitude? Has the individual always performed poorly? If not, why is he performing poorly now?

It is important to ask a manager or department head why his performance is below a more senior manager's expectations. This should be done privately and confidentially, and perhaps not in the senior manager's office, which may viewed as threatening or where the conversation may be more likely to be interrupted. Once a senior manager suspects that one of his team members is performing below par, it makes sense to document the circumstances. This documentation should be a part of a regular, formal, and fair evaluation process.

As a senior manager, ask yourself whether you could be part of a team member's performance problem? Have you made clear the kind and level of performance expected and how the project is expected to be accomplished? Did the team member agree to this standard? If you do not trust the team member, what facts can be marshaled in support of your judgment? Ask the team member if there is any way you, as a senior manager, can be more helpful.

Managers should expect those who report to them to respond differently to criticism, no matter how developmentally the criticism is meant. Some will agree with the evaluating manager on the facts, deny any generalizations, explain what went wrong, and promise to do better in the future. Others will disagree with the evaluator as to the facts or regarding their interpretation. Some will disagree on the definition of acceptable performance. Others will claim that outward events over which they had no control interfered with their performance.

After the manager and the team member have discussed the situation, the team member can come to one of several conclusions. The team member can accept the criticism constructively and attempt to change behavior. Generally speaking, it is easier to stop or to start doing something than to change doing something. The more specific a goal, the easier to know whether the team member can meet it. There is little a team member can do when accused of having a bad attitude; it is easier to initiate fewer conversations with certain staff members than to change the tone of those conversations.

It is important that the manager communicate to the team member that criticism is not meant personally; rather, the manager is attempting to be helpful so that the team member can meet the goals that both agree on. The team member must first genuinely perceive that there is a problem. If the manager perceives there is a problem, then a problem exists, even if the team member is blameless. (Of course, the manager should ask himself whether he is, to any extent, possibly contributing to part of the problem.) In disclosing concerns with team member performance, the manager runs the risk that, rather than changing behavior, the team member will withdraw and cover up, steadily arguing for lower managerial expectations and blaming outside influences if such expectations are not met.

It is at this point that the manager must act to get rid of the team member. If the manager lacks specific documentation, the alerted team member may be careful not to give the manager any specific reasons for dismissal. Reasons can always be manufactured, but the situation will have become decidedly unpleasant. Sometimes a situation is unavoidable, if only because the manager wishes to give each member of the team a fair chance.

A more useful approach may be to accept that, even if a team member has certain abilities, the manager and the team member have "a personality conflict." This may stem from different beliefs about organizational policy or style — a problem for both individuals that should be discussed calmly, if at all possible, to see what can be done. If there is a serious conflict, the two individuals have several choices: Either or both can resign. They can deny the problem, insist that each can meet mutual expectations, and attempt to do so. They can work to undermine each other. In this situation, the manager usually tells the team member that, if he does not wish to resign, the manager will fire him, first making sure, of course, that she has the ability to do so. The manager must be able to trust team members on whom she and others in the organization rely, and the manager cannot trust the team member when basic personality conflicts exist between the team member and manager or when there are major differences regarding organizational priorities or ways of conducting business.

The whole process may seem decidedly unfair from the point of view of the team member, department head, or administrative staff member, but injustice is sometimes a management reality. Managers are paid and respected for being able to deal effectively with risk and uncertainty. Loyalty to superiors is expected. There is no shortage of candidates for managerial positions, and top managers themselves are often asked to resign or are fired. Managers must be humane, remembering, "There, but for the grace of God, go I."

Sometimes being asked to resign or even being fired is the best thing that can happen to a team member (or to a manager). The position might never have worked out. A new job opportunity may turn out to be a promotion. Even if a new job pays less, working conditions may be better and the individual involved may feel more secure. A team member may be relieved at no longer having to attempt to perform in a certain way or to get along with a manager when neither was really feasible given the manager's and the team member's differing skills, beliefs, and experience. Team members may learn what their strengths and weaknesses at work are, how others perceive them, who their friends are, and what it is they really want to do. They may, in the process of changing jobs, strengthen ties with family and friends.

In the process, team members may learn how to avoid an avoidable termination, and this knowledge may enable them to do better similar or different work someplace else. Of course, some people never learn, and others are never given a second chance.

REORGANIZING A MANAGEMENT TEAM

A new manager is given three envelopes by the previous manager and is instructed to open one each time the new manager encounters difficulties on the job. Things are not going well, and the new manager opens the first envelope. The message inside reads, "Blame things on your predecessor." As working conditions worsen, the manager opens the second envelope. The message inside reads, "Now is the time to reorganize." As the situation continues to deteriorate, the manager opens the third envelope. The message reads, "Prepare three envelopes."

Reorganizing managerial responsibilities will probably not solve the most important problems the manager and the organization face, but this can give the manager time, at least, to better understand a current situation and identify key problems and concerns that stem from it. In this way, time is gained to respond more effectively to a situation.

Reorganizing is not always a cover-up for not having done things right in the first place. The external environment is constantly changing. New people join the organization, and team members leave who have been around and relied on for some time. When a member of the managerial team leaves, for whatever reason, it is a good time to reassess the vacated position. Ask whether the tasks and responsibilities that go with the job can be handled more effectively by someone else currently in the organization. Decide whether the manager herself should take over certain functions of the existing position, perhaps giving up certain other functions.

When a manager leaves, the position may stay vacant for a while, if only because the manager left suddenly and filling that kind of position takes a while. Leaving a position vacant for several months may be desirable to find out more about the former occupant's contribution and to specify any future occupant's potential contribution to organizational effectiveness and to the effectiveness of the team. The effects of a manager's leaving may not be noticeable, however, until considerable time has elapsed.

There are benefits and costs in reorganizing managerial responsibilities on a regular basis, even if the management team remains the same. A benefit is that each manager develops a clearer understanding of the total organization and of the problems faced by other managers on the team or in other parts of the organization. The organization becomes less dependent on specific managers because specific expertise is shared. Effective decision making may be facilitated because the team's judgment may become more balanced and involve different perspectives. Evaluation of managers is facilitated because a different manager may be the only significant variable that has changed to affect unit performance. Large organizations are able to rotate managers more frequently and give them greater career mobility within the organization, enhancing stability and breadth of managerial response throughout the organization.

On the other hand, while some managers like and can respond effectively to certain challenges, others do not like challenges—or certain challenges—and cannot respond well to them. If the manager is performing effectively, given his present responsibilities, why make a switch to do something he does not really want or know how to do? The manager may have spent years learning how to handle present responsibilities effectively; the manager may have earned the trust of peers and elicited outstanding performance from a number of carefully developed subordinates. In the new position the manager is likely to be ineffective, at least temporarily while learning new duties. Some managers work better meeting certain responsibilities and with certain subordinates than with others.

Small organizations have an advantage over larger organizations in that their managers tend to be less specialized; however, each manager's contribution may be relatively more important to superior organizational performance. A manager leaving or becoming incapacitated therefore tends to be a larger crisis for small organizations than for large organizations.

Example: Bob Bellows is director of the department of management information systems for Urban HMO, *which has 800,000 enrollees. Bellows reports to George Weiss, the vice president for hospitals and health centers. Wyatt Burns, the vice president for planning and support services, argues that Urban's management information systems department is many years behind current technology. Burns says his people are not getting the information they need, and that Weiss does not understand the problem and has ignored Burns's requests for overhauling management information systems.*

In response to Burns's complaints, Tim McGregor, the HMO *president, believes that if Burns would take over responsibility for directing information systems from Weiss, Burns would do a more competent job and would probably fire Bellows, who has worked loyally for the* HMO *for 11 years. However, Burns's proposed changes would cost a lot of money and result in a lot of temporary disruptions. Weiss would regard the shifting of responsibility as a slap in the face. McGregor is not convinced that the ineffectiveness of management information systems is as serious as Burns says for current* HMO *performance requirements. But McGregor admits that the system may well have to be upgraded significantly in the next three to five years.*

Reorganizing has important symbolic as well as substantive aspects for McGregor, Weiss, and Burns. It tells managers and subordinates which areas, units, or managers are considered problematic and are losing power and which are meeting managerial expectations and gaining power. If organizational responsibility for management information systems is shifted from Weiss to Burns, and if Burns can demonstrate improved performance and contribution to organizational effectiveness in the next two years, Burns will gain power relative to Weiss.

If, on the other hand, services deteriorate significantly after the change and after Burns has fired Bellows, or if Burns cannot demonstrate the department's enhanced contribution to organizational performance, Weiss will gain power relative to Burns. If HMO premiums have to be raised because of increased information system costs and because of decreases in the number of new enrollees, McGregor may downgrade Burns, even if the shift in managerial responsibilities had little to do with increased costs per member month. Burns may be extremely successful in reorganizing management information systems, leave the HMO, and found his own consulting firm. Does this leave McGregor and Urban HMO better or worse off?

When determining organizational changes, a review of the mission, vision, and values is appropriate. To the extent that a revised vision translated into goals and objectives can be used to drive organizational changes, it helps keep staff's focus in the right direction and minimizes personality issues.

WORKING WITH TEMPORARY ALLIES

Large organizations consist of many managers with different interests and dependencies on each other, who work with and against each other in shifting coalitions. In HMOs, temporary allies can include board members; physicians; managers of marketing, information, and medical affairs; other department heads; community officials; regulators; and managers in competing or allied organizations such as other HMOs, hospitals, and group practices.

Managers work together with temporary allies when their interests coincide. They work against each other when their interests conflict. They should be able to retain each other's trust and respect under changing circumstances by paying attention to each other as individuals, opposing each other without violating rules of courtesy, and committing themselves to what often becomes a slow, tedious, and inefficient process of decision making because of the need to pay sufficient attention to due process for all parties.

Issues on which temporary allies disagree can be categorized from the manager's perspective as important and not susceptible to compromise; important and susceptible to compromise; or unimportant. The manager can certainly give in or do nothing about issues in the first and third categories. The manager can attempt to gain additional allies or gain great influence over temporary allies through persuasion or inducement based on the manager's authority as an expert, or the manager can try to shift attention or alter perceptions. The manager can do all of the above, but he will destroy trust and respect by publicly agreeing with opponents and privately working against them.

What the manager has going for him in working with temporary allies is his organizational legitimacy as a manager. Managers are supposed to act in ways to meet their responsibilities to their superiors and their organization's goals. Managers coordinate organizational activities and people. Managers should have the time, information, and focus necessary to build effective coalitions. The manager's positions as organizational spokesperson and coordinator are subject to challenge, however, by those who may have the power to remove the manager or to curb managerial power. Others may perceive the manager as being merely an additional participant or interest group within the organization and as being ineffective. They may view the manager as being paid not to make problems (if that is how they view the manager's attempts to enhance organizational effectiveness) but to avoid or alleviate problems, that is, to provide support for the others' views and interests and to get out of their way.

When the manager is uncertain as to what her responsibilities really are or as to what will actually result from either action or inaction on her part, she must pay careful attention to communication, especially in communicating with persons who, because of different interests, may not trust her. Temporary allies are constantly seeking clues as to where managers really stand, what they really think, and how such managers really feel about them. Many such allies have primary interests outside of the organization, such as taking care of patients in their own offices, running businesses, or regulating other organizations. Thus, many issues that are important to one manager will be unimportant to others, and vice versa. The manager and temporary allies may be able to accomplish a great deal together, so long as they do not interfere with what each may think is very important.

When the manager is doing what she is supposed to be doing, it may be easier for those opposing the manager's policy or strategy to avoid the issues and attempt to discredit the manager personally. When others view the manager as not to be trusted, they will certainly oppose the manager's policy and strategy. If the manager is not trusted, she will have to spend an extraordinary amount of time documenting and communicating views and approaches and explaining why others should not fear her attempts. Certainly, given the power structure of most healthcare organizations, most managers cannot allow themselves to be mistrusted by many important stakeholders. If a manager cannot convince temporary allies to see things her way, she must at least persuade others that she is honest and predictable and that she understands their concerns. The manager cannot achieve this unless she spends time with others, listens to them carefully, and demonstrates by her behavior that their concerns matter to her.

MANAGING FAMILY

Example: *Dwight Robbins, administrator of the Henry Poor Neighborhood Health Center is highly esteemed for his managerial contribution by Cal Calderone, the CEO of Highsmith Hospital. However, Calderone has become aware that Robbins is absent from work frequently now that his wife Marlene has become a full-time doctoral student. Robbins has child care responsibilities that take up a lot of his time. When Calderone discussed the matter with Robbins, Robbins responded that he does his job; he must be absent on occasion; and that he plans to continue to be absent when one of his children is ill and his wife cannot stay home on certain days of the week.*

Contrast Robbins with Claire Rogers, director of nursing at Highsmith Hospital. Her husband, Henry, is a tremendous asset in Rogers's work. He supports her and is knowledgeable about her job. Henry is a gracious host and spends a considerable amount of time with the spouses of nurses who have recently started working at the hospital. Henry is active in local politics and is friendly with local businessmen, which has resulted in several donations to the hospital.

The manager's spouse, children, parents, siblings, friends, lovers, and ex-spouses are part of his managerial team because they affect how others view him, how he functions, and how he feels about himself. Spouse and children can provide the manager with support, respect, and love. Child care responsibilities can complicate and dilute performance at work. The manager's spouse or parents may have negative feelings about the manager's work or job or about persons with whom the manager works. Particularly when both spouses work and have school-age children, substantial conflict may exist between career ambitions and emotional needs.

Busy managers often find it difficult to devote sufficient time to family members. It is one thing not to be married, or to be married but not to have children and to work 70 hours a week, 50 weeks a year, for several years. It is another to do so when the manager's spouse works, when they have three preschool and school-age children, and when the manager has made a geographic change because of an important promotion.

Family can be of tremendous assistance in launching and fostering a managerial career. If the manager is working in a small town and his spouse's family is well-known and well-regarded, others will be more likely to trust the manager because they feel that the manager's local roots will cause him to take their values into account when making and implementing important decisions. Social relationships can significantly affect managerial careers. Although jealousies and antagonisms among workers' spouses are notorious for adversely affecting work relationships, cooperative and supportive relationships can work just as effectively in a positive direction. Friends made through volunteer work in the community can also help. Managers earn trust by helping others when there is nothing obviously to be gained by the manager. By helping others attain their own objectives, the manager may find it easier to induce others to help the organization or dilute potential negative reactions to what the manager or the organization is doing or planning.

Interacting with people in the community is a useful way for managers to get important feedback about how an organization is viewed by those who use and do not use its services. Persons not directly involved in the politics of the manager's organization may be more objective about the quality and availability of services or why certain groups of persons use or do not use a facility or program.

Managing healthcare is probably a poor career choice for persons who cherish privacy. This is not to say that some managers cannot be successful both at work and at leading separate, private lives away from the job. However, managers work longer hours than most other people and they are likely to have more work-related responsibilities to carry out after working hours. Away from work, especially in smaller communities, people will tend to view the manager first as what he is on the job and only second as a private person. Often the healthcare organization is one of the largest local employers, making the manager very visible. If the manager likes socializing, a managerial job can obviously be advantageous. Officials of community organizations will tend to respect the manager's position and look to him for participation in civic and charitable affairs.

For most, work is no substitute for loving relationships—and such relationships usually cannot endure without adequate time and energy devoted to them. Some managers may not be capable of loving relationships or may find them less important. For others, such relationships may develop and endure even if very little time is spent on them.

Probably too many managers spend too little time with their loved ones, and their relationships suffer because of it. Considering the extra hours that many managers work, more managers should take time off during regular working hours. Also, managers should consider taking vacations with those they love in places far away from work. Some managers enjoy taking spouses to work-related meetings or conventions; for others, doing so means either devoting inadequate attention to the work at hand or to the spouse.

Most people require private time and periods of complete rest both to revive themselves and as an opportunity to think deeply about their work. In what directions does the manager want to devote more or less effort? How can the manager's and the organization's goals be better accomplished? What does the manager want to accomplish at work, when, and where? Such thinking time can be gained by blocking out half days, full days, or weeks on the manager's calendar or by taking long walks or driving long hours before or after work. In any case, thinking time is valuable, and managers should build enough of it into their schedules.

7
Managing the Work

It all puts pressure on the core, a pressure which could be summed up by the new equation of half the people, paid twice as much, working three times as effectively...

— Charles Handy, *The Hungry Spirit,* 1998

THERE IS A TRANSITION TAKING PLACE in healthcare, the transition from a cottage industry to an industry of multiple networks. Joint ventures, alliances, mergers, acquisitions, and challenges from the government make managing a healthcare organization in a volatile and regulated environment a unique challenge. Hospitals are only now developing some influence over their medical staffs, that is, those who act as a sales force and define the use of the hospital's resources.

The view we will take in this chapter will encompass several different perspectives. We will examine the work from the view of a CEO looking at an entire organization and influencing its culture and vision. We will discuss a department manager's need to find better and more cost-effective ways to manage her department. We will explore a vice president's challenge of managing her budget in a time of declining resources. And last, we will explore the concerns of a board of trustees' chair when looking at the quality assurance program in a hospital.

MANAGING FROM THE TOP

Example: *Harold Staver, Midtown Hospital's new* CEO, *had been in his new hospital only three weeks when he was called out of a meeting to greet the unannounced surveyor from the Joint Commission, who planned to spend the next two days reviewing all the systems in the hospital. The executive group Staver inherited included a* CFO *and* COO *who had served three other* CEOs. *The newly appointed nurse executive was academically inclined, had a strong sense of nursing's leadership needs, and was quite independent. The* COO, *with a master's degree in hospital management, was crisis-oriented. The line managers had tenures ranging from two to twenty years.*

The medical staff leadership served both Midtown and the affiliated university hospital. The leadership was typically the chair of the department, often with split loyalties. Two key physician leaders were the outgoing and incoming presidents of the medical staff. Both were supportive and committed, believing that Midtown could function at a higher level, both in terms of its patient care activities and its medical education mission.

At the end of the two-day surprise survey, Midtown was placed on "tentative non-accreditation" for lack of compliance with Joint Commission guidelines.

The issues that arise from the above example are as diverse as the hospital itself: the quality of the clinical services; the relationship of the clinical leadership to management and their commitment to the hospital; the need to build a new team; the impact of graduate medical education programs; and the need to take control of the hospital's destiny.

The key to the management of clinical activities is the development of a system that collects data in a regular and routine fashion. This data is then presented to the clinical leadership in a manner that makes the conclusions obvious to all. A plan of action should follow, and management must ensure that this process takes place. Clinical leadership, whether in a teaching environment such as Midtown or in a community hospital, will be focused in other directions. The physicians are looking at individual patients and how the hospital systems support direct patient care activities. It is up to management to describe clearly the broader picture, complete with concrete data on trends and issues. The medical staff is scientifically trained and, therefore, responds to well-organized and well-presented information.

Ongoing discussions are now taking place about the role of accrediting organizations and how they will ensure quality healthcare services. It is not clear how the debate will be resolved. However, it is clear that a method of evaluating clinical services and examining each organization and its clinical outcomes will evolve. This evaluation process may be internal or external, but the manager must design and maintain a system that provides the necessary information both to the board and medical staff leadership.

As you can see from the Midtown Hospital example, taking on a new assignment is one of the greatest and potentially most rewarding challenges in a manager's career. This is true for all management levels in an organization, even though this example focuses on the CEO of a large, complex setting. The single biggest mistake consistently made by a manager in a new situation is underestimating the issues and relationships that already exist. If the issues appear straightforward, then the manager is probably missing something, and that something can come back to create troublesome problems.

You may be viewed as one more in a long line of managers who put their egos before the needs of the patients. So, not only must you take on the operational and program difficulties of your organization, you must also overcome the tendency of the medical and managerial staff to see you as transient.

It may be important that you not act too quickly. It is critical that you establish relationships while simultaneously attacking the operational concerns. Staver focused positive attention on the activities of others rather than on himself.

The environment is rapidly changing, and staff members have to see that they have an opportunity to manage their own destiny rather than be swept away by forces beyond their control. Many people have difficulty seeing that they have the power to influence their own environment. Frequently, middle managers are so caught up with day-to-day problem solving that they never take a step back and see where their influence can be directed. A major shift in the culture of the hospital in favor of action and taking responsibility will move the organization toward success.

Putting decision making at the lowest possible level in the organization and rewarding staff for taking risks to solve problems in new ways — not necessarily economic — can make a substantial difference.

Goal congruence in any work group will make successful implementation of change substantially easier. The starting place for this is an easily understood vision that can become the basis for action plans across the organization. The following is the process that Staver used as he guided Midtown through a turn-around process. He began with the key senior management and physician leadership in a retreat format.

The results of the retreat were brought back to the hospital and shared with a group of 30 top and middle managers. The discussions with this group paralleled the retreat discussions. These 30 were asked to buddy with one another to take the discussions back to their home departments and stimulate discussions. The cross-fertilization was conceived to ensure the consistency of the message to the entire hospital family. In reality, it resulted in interdepartmental activities that pushed Staver's goals beyond the original concept. Staff from the matched departments began sharing problems and, more importantly, solutions. Members of the medical records staff switched jobs with emergency room registrars to understand each other's problems better. The loading dock staff began making rounds on the nursing units to make sure their work was meeting the needs of the nurses. The department heads who brought their staffs together saw more opportunity to share ideas and solutions in an integrated manner.

At this point, the medical staff became quite interested in what was going on and wanted to be included, giving Staver the opportunity to invite them into the process and join the group of 30. They were surprised at the level of energy and enthusiasm being generated. The physicians saw a hospital-wide effort being made for everyone's benefit. The first sign of this understanding was a willingness on the part of the medical staff to fulfill the specific requirements of the Joint Commission and work with management to produce the required actions.

Taking a job in a different organization or a new assignment in your own organization will present unique opportunities. You will need to remove the barriers that impede your staff. You must help them think about their work in new ways, and help them learn to solve problems across departmental lines while keeping the organization's mission in mind. Most healthcare organizations have traditionally been organized in strict functional lines. To be successful today, those lines must disappear. Your job will be to assist your staff in making that happen.

You must get to know your operation as completely as possible, from a budget/financial perspective, from a staffing perspective, from a patient's perspective, and from a technical perspective. With this information, you can assist your staff in asking questions about how things can be done better. Who can they turn to within the organization to get more collaboration? What other issues are affecting their activities and vice versa?

Underlying these questions is the goal of improving the quality of service that the organization provides to all your customers. Whether the customers are the patients, the physicians, the other hospital staff, or the person in the next office, they are all looking to you and your activities to be consistent and supportive.

Table 7.1 summarizes the effect of Staver's activities.

PRODUCTIVITY

Every manager is faced with the need to reduce or control costs, particularly in the area of salaries and associated expenses. What is a reasonable level of expectation for staffing and productivity for the various areas of a hospital? Where does the operating manager look to get some guidance in setting standards and implementing changes?

Data Needs

A successful healthcare executive has been quoted as saying, "In God we trust. Everyone else bring data." What data are needed, where do they come from, who generates them, who interprets them, how accurate are they, and where can they be validated? These are all questions you must deal with when making a decision or presenting an argument in favor of a decision you support.

Table 7.1   Impact of Staver's Activities

Area of Action	Pre-Staver	Post-Staver
Accreditation	Midtown was under focused review by Joint Commission in several areas.	Successfully completed full Joint Commission review with recommendations for distinction.
Employee education and training	Human resources function was a processing area only.	Customer-focused orientation with new training for all staff. Managers were learning new skills and experiencing success.
Establish clear goals	Goals were to minimize problems for the city—both health and economic problems.	Developed goal congruence with management and medical staff for patient care and education.
Institutional pride versus institutional myth	"This is the Midtown Way!"	The "Midtown Way" became a symbol of quality services.
Managing the business	Solve problems by crisis management rather than fixing them.	Put attention on managing the process of providing services to the patients.
Physician accountability	House staff managed the patients with limited faculty participation.	Faculty became part of the planning and the implementation of improved care.
Strategic planning	Limited because of the city's interest in controlling future.	Expanded by focusing on what Midtown could control on its own.
Staff morale	Low, waiting for others to solve the problems.	Empowered staff to take action to improve services.

Data sources within an organization range from the robust to the rudimentary. It is outside our scope to discuss the development of information technology in healthcare and the organizations that deliver and pay for it. However, the need for detailed information is critical if substantial change is to take place. If you cannot measure it, you cannot consistently effect change.

Example: *Sharon Reading, director of registration, was a member of a performance improvement team to reduce bad debts at City Hospital. The team identified registration as the first measurement point in the billing process. Reading and her staff began tracking error rates in obtaining patients' specific information. The first report showed a 56 percent accuracy rate. Within two months, it had increased to 93 percent.*

Data sources can be the routine financial reporting information on a departmental or organization level, volume, and update information describing numbers of procedures, admissions, patient days, encounters, and length of stay. These data do not become meaningful until they are combined with a measure of the resource being used (input divided by output equals a measure of productivity). Reading was comparing accurate registrations divided by total registrations. She was also asked to look at worked hours divided by registrations and compare that calculation with that of a peer group (other hospitals) over a period of time. Managerial measures are generally straightforward and the associated benchmarks are available from a variety of sources: data services, consultants, sister organizations, and trade associations.

How to measure clinical outcomes has been a debate for many years. Standard measures are readmission rates, infection rates, adverse drug reactions, days in intensive care, as well as a variety of cost measures used as a proxy for clinical outcomes.

The manager's role is to assist the clinician in capturing meaningful data and presenting them in a manner that allows a conclusion to be drawn. This conclusion should identify a needed change in the process (e.g., different pharmaceuticals, improved ventilator management, new imaging equipment).

Downsizing

Example: *Terry Angelo, director of environmental services, was directed to find an 8-percent staff reduction in her department to meet industry benchmarks. Angelo felt the reduction could be accomplished with some significant changes in the management of the department. However, the changes would affect every member of the staff, putting them under a tremendous amount of pressure.*

It is not unusual for the goals and needs of an organization to conflict with the abilities of individual staff members. The issues raised in this example deal first with the continuing need for cost containment and then with practices reflecting the culture of a hospital.

Both the reduction in cost and the implementation of cost-containment systems are critical elements in managing how resources are expended. As a manager, you must be as prudent as possible with the resources you command. The demands on you will always exceed your ability to respond. However, the better you control the use of your resources—human, technical, material, or financial—the more flexibility the organization will have to respond to changing environmental pressures.

Managing resources and managing quality are not incompatible. Angelo was developing a quality product while containing her costs. As efforts to reduce costs continued, Angelo was able to improve the quality of the service. For example, Angelo found that women dusted and did the "high" work while men mopped and buffed the floors. This delineation of work by gender meant that too many workers were involved in the same activity. Following discussions with the union and some of the involved workers, Angelo reassigned the work to do away with these differences in job descriptions.

It took six months for the transition to take place. The women were given lighter mops and were asked to teach the men how to do the "high" work. The hospital purchased automatic floor scrubbers to replace most of the heavy mopping. One year later, the women were still shaking their heads as Angelo walked down the hall. However, there had been cost savings of 12.5 percent in the operation of the department and improvement in cleanliness as noted in the hospital's quality control system.

The supervisory staff was replaced with more knowledgeable and energetic people. Angelo was meeting with the staff to explain the department's new philosophy and the hospital's new expectations. The union was apprised of the intended increase in supervision and expectations.

Almost immediately, several staff workers who had viewed work as a social activity retired. Several more indicated an interest in exploring disability leaves. Several others decided to attempt to sabotage the new program by intimidating the supervisors. Hazardous waste was disposed of improperly, making the hospital vulnerable to fines. Several of the supervisors found the air let out of their tires, and Angelo received late-night anonymous phone calls.

In the end, the environment of the hospital improved dramatically, with reduced expense. A series of random checks against a benchmark established by the employees showed a consistently high level of cleanliness throughout the facility. And, more importantly, the staff's attitude toward their work improved noticeably.

Management will be consistently challenged to provide quality service to patients and staff in cost-effective ways. Concern over the quality of services and the cost to the purchasers will not abate. Managers must remain focused on the organization's mission as they change the organization's structure.

GENERATING RESOURCES

Changes cannot take place through the work of management alone. It must result from the integration of ideas and actions of all members of the work force. In the example above, the challenge was to change the behavior of the existing staff to upgrade the service. Old habits and patterns had to be unlearned. In many circumstances, these patterns had been learned in academic programs as well as on the job. They are not restricted to the housekeeping department but can be found in every department in the hospital.

As a new manager addressing changing pressures, you will be asked to create new modes of practice with the assistance of your staff and co-workers. The role of the manager is to act as the facilitator, communicator, and expeditor, not as the solo problem solver.

As we see changes occurring in the work force and the staff seeking more control over their own destiny and their work, management must create an environment—and generate resources—in which change can take place.

It is not only the dollar resources that are required to make changes happen. In many cases the economic support is available with an improvement in current spending patterns. But it is harder to provide and sustain the energy of the management and their consistent focus on improving performance and quality. The work force will often raises issues of "morale" as they are asked to change the way they do business.

If management is focused on making a difference and providing the leadership resource, the organization can be successful at implementing and sustaining change.

DIVERSITY IN THE WORK PLACE

Example: *Mildred Eng, nursing aide, was on her way into a patient's room when Gina Garofolo, a coworker, yelled greetings to her from down the hall. Mildred cringed; she felt like she was being criticized again. Gina smiled as she entered her patient's room. She liked Mildred and was happy to have said hello, even from a distance.*

How can management focus a diverse work force on creating new service-oriented and cost-effective ways of delivering nursing care? You will hear this question many times throughout your career. In the above example, Eng comes from a culture where loud communication means criticism. Garafolo, on the other hand, grew up in a family where loud communication was common. The beginning of a small but potent wedge in the work force can limit the manager's ability to effect a customer-focused service.

It is clear that without the active participation of the staff in the design of a new organizational structure, any redesign of jobs — combining or restructuring — will fail. The changing make-up of the work force must be handled creatively. Many organizations have added a "cultural diversity" component, however shallow, to their orientation program and have extended it to their managers. If the managers do not understand the nature of their work force, change becomes an impossible task.

Management has to be willing to establish the environment for experimentation to take place and to tolerate the risk of it not succeeding. Management has to be visible in its support of the experiment and provide the resources necessary for it to succeed, including staff training as well as financial support.

The concept of a broad level of participation in the creative problem-solving process will be the core of a successful organization in the future. Whether this approach follows a patient-focused organization or some yet-to-be-named organizational structure is not the issue. What will ultimately make a difference will be the satisfaction of the staff and their interaction and participation with the patients and other members of the healthcare team.

QUALITY

Example: *Marguerite Brown, chair of the board of trustees of Urban Medical Center, sat in the office of Barney White, the chief executive officer, discussing the activity in the hospital's quality assurance program. Neither was pleased with the response from the medical staff. Their concern centered on issues ranging from incomplete medical records to lack of consistent supervision of the rotating house staff. Both Brown and White were concerned about driving the medical staff away to other hospitals, but they were also aware that the existing behavior patterns could not continue. White had recently been queried by new board members about their responsibility for the quality of the healthcare being provided at Urban.*

The role of management in designing and implementing an effective quality assurance program that meets the needs of the board, the medical staff, the regulatory agencies, and, most importantly, the patients is one of balance, persistence, and diplomacy. You are asking physicians, who generally wish to be independent, autonomous practitioners, to prove to a group of lay directors that the medical care provided is appropriate and consistent with good medical practice. The quality assurance literature has debated the best way to evaluate care for many years. In the late 1980s, the notion of continuous quality improvement, or total quality management, began creeping into the healthcare literature and practice.

In general, there are three approaches to evaluating quality. The first is a measure of the outcomes of the care rendered, such as the caesarean-section rate in an obstetrics department. A significant debate remains as to the industry's ability to define outcomes precisely enough to make this a meaningful tool. However, more research is being conducted on outcomes today, and it is likely that within the next few years major emphasis will be placed on examining outcomes as a quality measure.

The second approach is to use process measures as a proxy for the quality of care rendered. Have all the appropriate steps been taken to provide the necessary care to the patient? Is the medical record complete? Is it timely? Is there evidence of supervision of the house staff? Is there a process in place to review the quality of the information written in the medical record? And, of course, is there a mechanism to report the findings of these reviews to the decision-makers and the board of the hospital?

The third and most recently embraced approach is the use of a continuous quality improvement process to monitor and improve the patient care services. This approach is based on W. Edwards Deming's work in quality control[25] and has been incorporated into the standards of the Joint Commission.

In the actual implementation of a quality assurance program, all three approaches must be incorporated. They may be used to look at different parts of the organization or different functions within the same department, including the clinical and nonclinical areas of the healthcare organization. Consumers are most concerned about the outcomes of the clinical quality, but they also want to be assured that the room they are using is clean, that they can get to their radiology appointment on time, and that when they get there they will be treated courteously and competently.

In contrast to the outcome and process systems, the continuous quality improvement approach asks: What are the important aspects of the service being provided? Can these aspects be translated into quantifiable terms? Can they be measured? If so, can they be tracked over time to develop a pattern of activity reflective of the work being performed, indicating where improvements need to be made?

The example focused on the information required by the board to make informed decisions about the quality of services provided by the hospital. Intimidated by their lack of clinical knowledge, most boards feel uneasy about having to judge the quality of the clinical service provided by their hospitals.

It is the role and responsibility of management to gather, synthesize, and report in a clear, logical fashion the quality measures of the services being provided. This responsibility extends to the entire range of the institution's services, not simply the clinical activities.

The director of admitting and the chief engineer must develop a set of standards applicable to their areas in the same manner that the medical and nursing staffs develop standards to measure their performance. However, do not lose sight of the effect of a physician's misjudgment as compared to that of a registrar. Most institutions have elaborate reporting systems for unusual incidents in both areas. However, the problems of a water leak or a disabled elevator seem to get reported instantly to the senior manager, while clinical issues often make their way through the reporting system at a slower pace.

We shall not describe the pros and cons of the various methods of quality assurance and continuous quality improvement. There are many excellent sources for that information. For our own purposes as developing managers, we are concerned with understanding that there is a process in place that meets our organization's needs.

Management must assist the board by directing its questions to all the parties in the hospital, especially to the medical staff. Similarly, management must assist the medical staff in the identification of critical indicators for their activities. Herein lies a major challenge for the management staff. Few physicians will eagerly point out the critical points in their service. You must be persistent and persuasive to obtain their cooperation in this effort. Fortunately, hospital managers have three powerful tools.

The first is the board itself. Most hospital boards are quite aware of their liability for the activities within the hospital and are not inclined to tolerate much obfuscation from the medical staff.

Second, the Joint Commission has promulgated standards addressing quality assurance and continuous quality improvement. Most of the medical staff understand the importance of maintaining the hospital's Joint Commission accreditation. If they do not, you have one more educational task in front of you.

Third, all three branches of government—executive, judicial, and legislative—have addressed the requirements of the hospital, its board, and its medical staff with regard to quality of service.

These tools can be persuasive in encouraging the medical staff to participate in the development of their own monitoring standards. In addition, the professional organizations, such as the American College of Surgeons and the American College of Obstetrics and

Table 7.2   Before and After Implementing Quality Management

Existing System	Revised System
Individual behavior	Team functioning
Focus on problems	Focus on patterns
Look for blame	Look for continuous improvement
Crisis orientation	Establish feedback mechanisms
Short-term impact	Aim for long-term behavior

Gynecology, have nationwide committees developing guidelines and indicators.

Your role as a manager is to present your knowledge of the process required to identify the critical issues that need monitoring in each department. You must determine how this information is monitored, collected, trended, reported to the department, acted on, reported to the medical staff, reviewed, reported to the board, reviewed again, and sent back to the original department for follow-up. This process becomes a closed loop, with continuous feedback to the board and the clinicians and with continuous corrective action taken as necessary. Table 7.2 describes the situation before and after a new manager addresses the continuous quality improvement needs of a hospital. This type of system can be shared with the board of directors and can serve as a basis for their questions. In addition, the board must be assured that there is an ongoing and consistent process in place. Once it is clear that the indicators are developed and data are being collected, you must ascertain how often the data are examined and if they are being used to make decisions about changing practices, changing levels of privileges, or changing educational activities for the attendings or house staff.

The board can review the process that any department uses to collect data. It can also review the use of that data. If information is collected but does not indicate any atypical outcomes, then the board must ask if the indicators are precise enough. For example, if there are 2,000 deliveries at the hospital every year and there are no issues that arise from the physician monitoring process, it may be time to redefine the criteria or move on to new indicators.

Another area the board should be interested in is the basic credentialing process of the physicians. In the 1990s, there was a great deal of discussion about laser and laporoscopic surgery. Both of these techniques have been highly visible in the popular press, and many surgeons would like to market themselves as performing them. The hospital and its board must be assured that the surgeons taking on these procedures are appropriately trained and credentialed.

It is the board's role to question management and the medical staff about the process being used to ensure that physicians have the proper training and supervision to perform new procedures—prior to the actual performance of the procedure. The documentation of the credentialing process, as well as the assurance of a regular review, is what a board can and should be monitoring. Management must be prepared to present this information to the board and to assist the medical staff in carrying out the credentialing process.

SUMMARY

In this chapter, we have described a series of situations taken from our own experiences in health services organizations, focusing especially on patient care activities. We discussed the manager's role in working with a board of directors, a medical staff, and other hospital employees.

We described the need to manage the quality of clinical services. The health services manager cannot lose sight of the product—caring for a patient. When the quality of the manufacturing process slips, the effect is substantially different than when the patient care process breaks down.

The hospital, the focus of these examples, is but one type of healthcare organization. The issues of managing clinicians, boards, and scarce resources are found in all HMOs, home health agencies, group practices, durable medical equipment companies, and long-term care organizations.

We have not attempted to deal with every issue, but rather to focus on a few that are more generic and widespread. The art of managing an organization, whether it is the housekeeping department at budget reduction time or the medical staff at Joint Commission accreditation time, will challenge your technical knowledge and your interpersonal skills. Each will present you with challenges and opportunities that may differ. Your concern will remain to be productivity, quality, and cost.

8
Working with Physicians and Other Clinicians

Building a flock with these sorts of high-priced eagles around is not going to be easy, but in life, as on a boat, one star does not make a great crew, unless that star is prepared to commit himself or herself to the common cause.

— Charles Handy, *The Hungry Spirit*, 1998

OUR BASIC APPROACH TO WORKING WITH clinicians in medical care organizations follows that of John Griffith: Medical care managers must develop relationships with physicians and nurses so that the community gets the medical care it wants; medical care should be the primary product or service provided by these organizations.[26] Managers must recruit and retain doctors and nurses and offer staffing plans that guarantee them adequate work and income, operation of a high-quality program, and the opportunity to associate with like-minded peers and to participate meaningfully in discussions affecting their mutual future. Where there is conflict, how to better serve the community is the mutual benefit decision criterion.

RULES OF THE GAME

As a general rule, physicians and other clinicians are intelligent and well-educated. The professional schools for medicine, dentistry, and nursing select from a large pool of bright applicants. This is not to suggest that doctors or other clinicians make good managers. In fact, the nature of their interests and training leads them along a different path. However, do not underestimate their ability to generate interesting ideas, challenge managerial decisions, and engage in political power struggles.

Information is power in every organization; you as a manager have access to or are able to generate significant amounts of data. If you are able to convert the data into easily understood information, you should be able to focus decision making with clinicians on a data-driven process rather than an emotional one.

The clinician's relationship to the formal organization is unique. In most cases, he is not an employee but an independent private practitioner operating a small business. He is committed to his own success and to professional colleagues, not to you or the hospital unless given a personal or other reason to do so. Clinicians also differ among themselves, depending on their specialty, their age, their practice location, and the current organization's investment in their services.

Responding to Complainants

"Perception is reality" is the key to understanding and dealing with issues raised by a medical staff. Their concerns tend to fall into three major categories: (1) what affects the patient and the patient's view of how care is provided; (2) what affects the physician's ability to practice efficiently; and (3) what the institution is doing in the community to assist the physician's ability to attract patients.

It is critical that operating managers respond promptly and comprehensively with solid information and action, if appropriate, to a physician complaint. The physician will continue to look to you as a responsive problem-solver if you can deal with the issues in a straightforward manner. This does not mean that the answer will always be what the physician wants. It does mean that you responded in a professional manner, collected the necessary information, initiated an appropriate action, and reported back in a timely fashion.

The most difficult situations arise when complaints shift from process concerns to personal issues, aimed either at you or another staff member. Resolution of these complaints may require assistance from your boss or a more senior clinician. It is imperative that you keep your boss well informed about all the issues concerning physicians and to call for assistance early enough to allow a solution to be implemented.

THE PHYSICIAN PERSPECTIVE

Since the advent of governmental health insurance (Medicare and Medicaid), there has been an unrelenting effort to control hospital and healthcare costs. Over time, this effort has begun to focus on the way physicians practice medicine. The growth of managed care on the West Coast and elsewhere has forced physicians to examine their practice patterns along with their resource utilization. By the mid-1990s, physicians were being pressured by hospitals, insurers, and patients to reduce costs, length of hospitalizations, and practice variations. You, the healthcare manager, are generally the bearer of cost-containment news. By association, you are seen by physicians as affecting their ability to practice medicine in an independent fashion. This has created a new level of tension between the physician and the manager.

Eliot Freidson asserts that many questions of medical care are social, not professional, questions, although they are not often addressed as such. Examples include information regarding alternative methods of treatment and the freedom to change treatment, patient convenience versus provider convenience, and decisions concerning institutionalization. For example, medical consultants may be used to provide legal protection for the physician without even asking the patient's permission.[27]

The point of the above is not to belittle or denigrate physicians. Many physicians do work well in organizations, provide care of adequate or superior quality, and cause managers little or no trouble. Perhaps these physicians should be causing managers more trouble, if that would mean ensuring better service to patients. Even if much of medical care is not cost effective, the treatment physicians provide is often valued greatly by patients, who continue to regard at least their own physicians highly. What is more important for managers to realize is that physicians and managers have legitimately different interests and that physicians are not always right about what they define as medical matters. Managers should enter the medical arena with extreme caution, but they must enter it occasionally, for this is where the stakes are often highest for the patient. Physicians' "buy-in" is often necessary for success with tasks and projects; frequent meetings and conversations can help obtain this "buy-in."

Physician Expectations

Physicians expect to be recognized for the important contributions they make to health services organizations and to American society (physician status in the United States is higher than that of health services managers or other professionals). Physicians expect managers to give due, and sometimes undue, consideration to their livelihoods and their egos.

Attending physicians usually earn more per hour for hospital services than for office services. A growing number of physicians are totally dependent on health services organizations for their remuneration.

Physicians guard their status relative to peers in their organization and in other organizations. They want to determine their own working conditions and will fight vigorously any decision that negatively affects "their" space, "their" equipment, or "their" personnel. Physicians require adequate support services to treat patients.

Physicians do not wish their time to be wasted or to spend more time at organizational meetings than is absolutely necessary. Most of them work at least 55 to 60 hours a week. Physicians, like everyone else, want to be consulted about policy decisions they feel will affect them, both before policy is made and during its implementation.

Managerial Response

If your employment is dependent in part on not antagonizing physicians, why not meet their expectations, many of which seem quite reasonable? To begin with, managers do not control the distribution of many of the organizational resources that physicians want and expect. Limited amounts are available. If every physician has similar access to you or to organizational resources, none of them is better off than any other. Some of them wish to be or deserve to be better off than others.

Financial pressures on the organization may cause a deterioration in the physician's working conditions. Paying customers may move out of a hospital's service area. Expenditure ceilings may be placed on the hospital by regulators. Physicians' interests often conflict with organizational goals or with the interests of other physicians. Trustees may wish to establish ambulatory services for the underserved poor and handicapped; attending physicians may oppose the services as potentially competitive with their private practices or as having the capacity to erode their incomes. Hospital service in ambulatory care, supervising house staff, or committee participation may require substantial amounts of time away from a remunerative practice.

Managers and physicians may have different concepts of productive time. The time physicians spend at committee meetings is time away from patient care and time for which they are not being paid, but managers are being paid and are performing their jobs properly when attending meetings. (The hourly rate of compensation tends to fall as more and longer meetings are attended after hours.)

Sometimes events move too quickly for you to consult adequately with certain physicians whom you would like to contact. Sometimes physician officials do not spend enough energy and time communicating with staff in their departments or on their committees. Sometimes staff physicians do not attend meetings that are organized for communicating with them or do not thoroughly read letters and memos that are sent to keep them informed.

Identifying and establishing alliances with key medical staff members often helps in communicating and building consensus. However, never assume that a positive communication with one physician will be transmitted to another. You must use every communication tool available to reach the broadest possible audience: individual face-to-face and group meetings, organized staff meetings, newsletters, and e-mail systems. The ability to sustain consistent and trusting relationships with the medical staff will be one of the defining elements of your tenure.

THE MANAGERIAL PERSPECTIVE

Given that managerial and physician goals sometimes conflict and that physicians may lack commitment to organizational goals, what kind of behavior do managers expect from physicians with whom they must deal on a regular basis?

Managerial Expectations

You may expect recognition for your position and your person if you are seen as helpful to the physician's interests. You may expect general commitment from physicians to organizational goals, at least to the extent prescribed in organizational bylaws and departmental and medical staff rules and regulations. You may expect physicians to fulfill certain organizational responsibilities, such as attending medical staff meetings or committee meetings that they chair. You may expect physicians who disagree with you on policy matters not to take it out on you personally (because your support may be necessary to them on other important issues). You may be permitted to discuss policy decisions made by medical officials when their decisions affect your responsibilities. Such decisions may concern appointment to and composition of medical staff committees or the slate of officers for the medical staff organization.

Physician Response

Example: *Dr. Seaver, a 53-year-old pulmonary specialist, appeared in the office of Ms. Elinor, CEO, slightly agitated and eager to talk. He had just learned from his accountant that his income had decreased 18 percent from last year. Seaver proposed that the hospital buy his practice and put him on a salary.*

If physicians are becoming increasingly dependent on the organizations in which they work, then why do they not meet managerial expectations more regularly? To begin with, physicians believe that the primary responsibility of managers is to support the physicians and nurses who take care of patients, rather than to coordinate activities among clinical and support services and to relate the organization to outside groups and organizations.

Through the early 1990s, hospitals were buying physician practices to control the admissions. Rarely did this yield the desired results. In Seaver's case, Elinor must assess Seaver's importance to the hospital. Is there any collateral benefit to the hospital for owning his practice? How would it be perceived by Seaver's peers? Can an incentive-based agreement be reached so that the hospital isn't merely replacing

Seaver's lost income? How does a practice purchase fit with the hospital's strategic plan? In all such agreements, a detailed analysis, due diligence process of the practice and its benefit must be conducted before a final decision is made.

Seaver and cohorts are experiencing a negative shift in their incomes, in contrast with what they had come to rely on for the previous two decades. As a result, they are turning to institutions for support and solutions. While managers must be respectful and understanding, they cannot be seen as the source of patient care revenue replacement.

Driven by the changing economics of healthcare, the shifting nature of physician and hospital relationships is putting new pressures on both parties. In addition to looking to you for patient care support, physicians are looking to you for your knowledge of the payment system. You are a representative of an organization with financial resources that can help them protect their incomes and their patient base. They are conflicted. They look to you for support, but at the same time suspect that you will seek control over their working conditions, income, and status. Such suspicions may be well-founded, especially as physicians become more plentiful and as managerial performance becomes more critical to the effectiveness of larger and more complex health services organizations.

Physicians may bitterly disagree with you on policy. They may feel that your "persuasion" of other physicians and trustees is unfair. They may believe that you unfairly interpret their principled opposition to managerial initiatives as personal attacks on you and that you communicate your interpretation to board members. In such circumstances, physicians may feel justified in attacking you personally—either to your face or behind your back—in the presence of other physicians and trustees. Physicians may have a direct conflict of interest with certain organizational goals. A surgeon may have ownership in a surgicenter and serve on the hospital board. An internist may refer all laboratory work to a competing for-profit laboratory. On the other hand, attending physicians may suffer financially when they devote too much time to hospital business. Their health or family life may suffer if, after accepting additional hospital responsibilities, they do not reduce the number of hours they spend in the office.

Many hospitals lack effective accountability systems for medical officials. For example, a chief of surgery may be elected to serve a one-year term on a rotational basis. Such a chief cannot be expected to hold other surgeons accountable for the quality of their work, their attendance at meetings, and so forth. The chief, in turn, may not be held accountable in any formal way to a higher hospital authority.

New organizational structures that include the medical staff (or parts of it) and the hospital may provide opportunities to bring the two parties together for business development that can benefit both the hospital and the physicians. The risk associated with "simple" business solutions is that most physicians, as small business owners, are focused on their own needs. Being able to broaden the physician's view as they gain an understanding of the limits on organizational resources is the challenge every healthcare manager must pursue.

INFLUENCING PHYSICIANS

Example: *Midcity Memorial's new* CEO, *Frank Sands, quickly recognized the need to focus the energies of the management staff and the physician leadership around a few key strategies, such as improving quality of care and cost containment. The physicians, hungry for influence and leadership, agreed to participate in a priority-setting planning process. For many of them, it was a first: being asked what the future should look like and how it should be attained.*

Sands established a strategic planning process with a broad range of medical staff members. With the help of a facilitator, a slate of strategic initiatives was established. Each initiative had a physician champion and medical staff task force and was coordinated by a senior manager. The task forces reported regularly to the board of trustees with plans and actions that guided Midcity for the next 18 months.

Not every planning effort was successful. The critical issues involved the consistent vision of the task force, the champion's ability to lead the effort in a collaborative fashion, and the manager's ability to keep the interests on track. If the task force members are in direct competition for scarce patient volume, the group's effectiveness will be limited.

The successful teams established new programs, recruited new physicians, extended services outside the traditional boundaries, and sought input from physicians, nurses, and other constituents.

Despite the inherent difficulties, there are compelling organizational reasons for trying to influence physician behavior. You must show good judgment. Worry about making too many decisions; worry about making decisions too soon or too late; but make decisions. If decisions will affect physicians, then by all means involve physicians, at appropriate levels, in implementation. Before making a decision, you must have the best facts available or be working to get them. Your reputation for honesty and trustworthiness is usually more important to physicians than your technical knowledge.

Do not promise more than you can deliver. Raising false expectations is dangerous and jeopardizes your credibility. If you make a mistake that you recognize before the physicians see it, acknowledge it. Often such actions can diffuse a potential challenge to you.

Charles Lindblom indicates three ways of influencing others: exchange, authority, and persuasion.[28] Physicians will go along with you on an issue in exchange for scarce resources of program commitment, space, budget, or personnel. You may do favors for physicians. As Robert Strauss, former chairman of the Democratic National Committee, has said, "Doing favors is like money in the bank." Always keep in mind, however, that physicians are less dependent on a hospital than they are on the good will of other physicians, who refer patients to them.

Physicians will not oppose you if they believe you have the relevant expertise or experience on a certain issue. They will agree with you on policy when you can persuade them that what you want them to do is in their best interest.

SOURCES OF PHYSICIAN POWER

Example: *It was 10:15 p.m. when Mary Francine, chief operating officer at Bellmore General, heard from her* O.R. *staff. Dr. Joseph Patrick had just declared as an emergency a broken hip seen in the* E.R. *and called for the* O.R. *team. Francine knew that the case would cost the hospital three times the normal expense and stress her staff. She had been through this before with Patrick.*

Physicians have several sources of power in dealing with managers. They may have certain legal rights, as stated in the organization's bylaws, medical staff bylaws, or contracts specifying the terms of their employment. By law, they are the only ones who can admit or discharge patients and make clinical decisions. Physicians often have substantial informal power because of their working relationship with nurses and technicians. Physicians often have direct access to important board members and community leaders, each of whom, after all, has a personal physician. Physician orders drive the allocation of hospital resources; physician admissions drive hospital revenues. Physicians have multiple relationships that affect the ways in which management deals with them. For example, hospital radiologists are members of the hospital medical staff. They may have their own management contract with the hospital. They may be members of the American Medical Association, the state medical association, and their own specialty association of radiologists. They are dependent on referrals for much of their income.

At Bellmore General, there was no chief of staff or chief of orthopedics willing to challenge Patrick. He was known for his clinical skill and volatile behavior. The COO, not a physician, had no success in dealing with Patrick and had no clinical leadership to back her. With growing economic concerns, a strong clinical manager, either a physician or nurse manager, with senior management support can make an important difference in resource utilization.

Saltman and Young[29] emphasize that physicians as a group maintain control over hospital decision-making processes by maximizing the uncertainty that they will perform their functions as expected. Physicians often have the power to admit their patients to other hospitals or to set up competing organizations, at least for the provision of ambulatory services.

A final source of power is the physician's technical knowledge. When a physician defines a situation as a medical emergency, managers jump now and ask questions later.

SOURCES OF MANAGEMENT POWER

Managers typically know a great deal more than physicians do about finance, regulation, accreditation, corporate planning, fund raising, personnel policy, and other operations in health services organizations.

They may be better prepared than physicians to systematically improve the quality of care to patients and to the community.

The executive officer of a not-for-profit hospital or an HMO is selected by a governing board and may enjoy special access to board members. Managers have access to information that is usually not available to or not easily understood by many physicians (in the amount of time they are willing to devote to interpreting such data). Data that physicians lack is available to managers about physician practice patterns and norms. Such data can be used to monitor physician activities. Hospital budgeting allocations, influenced by managers, shape physician practice options. Physicians see managers as cost cutters when they differ on allocation of resources.

Managers may have certain responsibilities because of their employment contracts (although most managers do not have such contracts) or because of the bylaws of the organization, such as membership on certain hospital board committees or on the board itself. In responding to physicians who want what you perceive to be inappropriate special considerations, you can often rely on other physicians who agree with you to see to it that such claims can be safely discounted as long as you are following appropriate procedures.

A major source of your power in dealing with physicians is that you are paid to manage and not to do anything else. You have the time and the resources to document carefully and thoroughly your opinions and positions. Your major weakness is that you are greatly outnumbered by physicians, who control the production process and who have legitimate interests in joining together to oppose management and other organizational or external groups.

THE ORGANIZED MEDICAL STAFF

One of the greatest challenges facing hospital executives is dealing with the organized medical staff. The medical staff organization typically includes a president and other elected officers. The medical staff organizes itself into committees that carry on its business. These committees reflect the preferences of the individual hospital staff, current issues, and Joint Commission and other regulatory-body requirements. The CEO is charged with working with and through the organized medical staff. The committee structure can be of great assistance in communicating with the various elements of the staff. However, the committees can also be a source of delay and opposition around difficult issues that the medical staff must address. It can obfuscate issues about medical care while spending time on managerial concerns. The CEO is usually the management representative to the medical board or executive committee. This governing group usually meets monthly and conducts the official business of the medical staff, which is then customarily reported to all attending physicians and to the board of trustees.

The medical board's other committees are staffed by other management staff members—an excellent opportunity for the less experienced manager to develop skills of working through committee structures, constructing appropriate agendas, establishing working relationships with physicians, and influencing hospital operations.

In providing staff support to a medical board committee, the manager should assist the physician chair in preparing the agenda, ensure follow-up of decisions made at the committee level, and take and draft the committee minutes.

ACCOMMODATING EACH OTHER

In communicating with physicians, stay calm, polite, and consistent unless some valid reason for acting otherwise arises. Your tone in conversation should be steady and never patronizing. Remember that physicians want to know what behavior they can expect from you. They want you to be on their side, particularly when they are "wrong." You must attempt to do what is "right" for the patient and the hospital, but you must also protect your job. Others should expect from you only what you as a manager, or what any other manager, can do in a given situation.

To work effectively with physicians, you must earn their trust, as well as that of the governing board leaders. Physicians must know that you take their interests into account when making decisions. You may be able to persuade physicians to give up a short-term interest now for some greater gain in the future, but often only if you can show them that not giving it up will cost them more. Stay focused and do not take on more issues than you can manage. Time may eventually prove your judgment to have been sound.

WORKING TOGETHER: SOME EXAMPLES

Examples of recurring problems that managers and physicians face are late completion of medical records, effective decision making on capital budgeting, and development and implementation of new service programs (or abandonment of ineffective or inefficient existing service programs).

Late Completion of Medical Records

A typical problem in short-term community hospitals is completion of medical records within a specified time. According to the Joint Commission *Accreditation Manual for Hospitals*, "the hospital maintains medical records that are documented accurately and in a timely manner, are readily accessible and permit prompt retrieval of information, including statistical data."[30] Prompt completion of medical records may be important to a hospital's cash flow because bills cannot be sent to third-party payors until physicians fill in their diagnoses. Hospital medical staffs have rules stating that records must be completed within a certain number of days after discharge.

Example: *Loss of admitting privileges is the penalty for late completion of records at Urban Community Hospital, a 250-bed general hospital affiliated with Urban HMO. About 20 percent of Urban Hospital's admissions are HMO patients. It is a fairly common practice for non-HMO physicians, many of whom have busy practices, to violate the rules and to keep admitting patients while they are "catching up" on their backlog of incomplete medical records, thus causing the hospital to lose considerable cash flow.*
"Why don't these physicians complete their medical records on time like the HMO physicians?" asks Tony Bullitt, administrator of Urban Hospital. Dr. Marshall says he is too busy taking care of patients and attending hospital meetings. Dr. Franklin dislikes completing medical records, believing it is not really a very good use of her time. Dr. Clyde

wants to know why someone else can't do more of the job or make it easier for him to complete his medical records, adding that last week the dictating equipment was broken and his wife, Thelma, was ill.

There is probably no acceptable solution to the problem of late and incomplete medical records. Every hospital is challenged by it and no solution works all the time. It is an example of a hospital's needs versus a physician's interest that management must resolve. Some efforts include medical record signing parties, delivering records to physicians' offices, providing a dictation system with a template for discharge summaries or operative notes, and jointly hiring a physician extender to do the dictation. One hospital raffled off $100 to all the physicians whose charts were up-to-date.

Capital Budgeting

The Joint Commission requires each hospital to have a three-year capital budget. The funds available for capital will depend on a variety of local and reimbursement issues. There is never enough capital available for all the medical and nonmedical needs in any organization.

Example: *The administrator of Highsmith Hospital, Cal Calderone, asks all physician chiefs and nonmedical department heads to make equipment requests for the next three years. He also asks them to classify requests as (1) emergent (for medical care reasons or because they are required by licensing and accrediting authorities) or money saving; (2) important and needed; and (3) nice to have. Category 3 is useful for requesters so that they will not forget to put these items on the list again the next year, perhaps in category 2. Physician chiefs and department heads are asked to document their priority requests by answering the question, In what ways, if any, does the requested equipment produce greater benefits or result in lower costs as compared with present equipment, if applicable?*

 From a political perspective, Calderone does not want to give certain physicians the opportunity to single him out as the reason why their equipment requests are being denied, especially if rival physicians' requests are being honored. He suggests that the board consider establishing dollar ceilings related to the amount external payors will allow. He asks the board chair to recommend that the board and the medical staff set and approve criteria for evaluating capital expenditure requests. His staff can assist chiefs in justifying future requests. As long as the medical staff participates in the allocation process, due process will be observed, and if the governing board sets a limit on the amount to be spent on medical equipment, Calderone feels that the capital budgeting process will be acceptable to most physicians. Whether there will be enough money to fund a sufficient amount of desired and agreed-on equipment requests is, of course, another matter.

Capital budgeting is a challenging activity for any organization. The level of available resources is never sufficient to meet every organizational need or physician wish. The process described in Calderone's hospital is typically just the beginning step of identifying what people are thinking about. After prioritization has taken place, a thorough economic analysis must be conducted. If the expenditure is a routine replacement, the analysis is straightforward. If, however, the expenditure is a major investment—such as a building, major remodeling, or cash-flow requirements—then a business plan should be developed describing the benefits and risks associated with the expenditure. Some organizations establish a minimum rate of return expected from any new investment (i.e., Can the project exceed what a conservative financial investment would generate?).

It is the manager's responsibility to do the analytic work necessary to understand the impact of the project or purchase.

Establishing New Services

The difficulty of implementing decisions that are in the organization's interest (as defined by board members) but not in certain physicians' interest should be clear by now. Board members can seldom marshal the necessary knowledge, will, and time, even with managerial support, to oppose a united group of physicians.

Example: *Hospital administrator Victor Allen wishes to start an elder care program at Glory Hospital. He believes that there is a community need (which researchers at nearby Eastern University are eager to validate), that start-up funds can be raised from philanthropic sources, and that operational funds can be obtained from some third-party payors. Dr. Benjamin Riggio, president of the medical staff, speaking on behalf of several staff physicians, raises objections to the program. "What's the hurry in getting the university in to study the need for this program? They are going to make us look bad, and accuse us of over-hospitalizing our patients. We don't agree with their methodology. Who needs this program anyway? Is the hospital planning to go into competition with the medical staff for these patients? We need to spend more money on medical equipment. The hospital doesn't belong in long-term care anyway. Frankly, if this program does well, some of the medical staff think you, Victor Allen, as the administrator are going to get too powerful."*

Mutual accommodation between physicians and managers may mean dropping this program at this time. It is generally unwise for managers to attempt to change the goals of a direct service organization whose production process is controlled by physicians who the manager does not control. Because of the political nature of these organizations, a successful leader must build a constituency for his or her point of view.

What are Allen's alternatives? He can discontinue efforts to start the elder care program; he can begin a lobbying effort with the medical staff leadership; he can push the board to accept the program against the medical staff's wishes in favor of a community need; or he can table the idea for a period of time. If Allen believes that the program represents a critical need in the community and that the hospital's success is linked to the community's needs, then he must develop a new strategy to carry it forward.

The example indicates that Allen fell out of sync with the medical staff by not understanding their view of the impact of the elder care program and by failing to find a way to articulate the benefit to both the physicians and the hospital.

A strategy to recover the thrust of the program would be to have a physician leader who likes the program help design a process whereby patient referrals would be shared by a broader group of medical staff members. An opportunity to link a number of physicians to the success of the program will benefit everyone.

INVESTING AND SPENDING POLITICAL CAPITAL

Example: C E O *Richard Frances had a decent working relationship with Dr. Greg Ortho, a member of the hospital's board of trustees. At the latest nominating committee meeting, it was recommended that fewer physicians be on the board in favor of a more active Joint Conference Committee. As a result, Ortho was not re-nominated. He was informed in a letter signed by the chairman of the board. The relationship between Frances and Ortho became overtly adversarial.*

Frances, who generally worked well with his physicians, was perceived by Ortho as arranging an end to Ortho's board term. Frances missed the opportunity to maintain good relations by allowing the communication with Ortho to be done by letter instead of a personal visit. As a result, a powerful enemy was created. Many physicians find it difficult to trust managers completely. Managers must try, therefore, to be seen as predictable, well-disposed toward physicians, and actively communicating with them. Getting physicians to regard you in this way is usually, like so many other things, the result of a great deal of hard work. You must invest in relationships by helping physicians solve their problems as they see them in ways that they find helpful.

Francis appointed Ortho to a few key committees including an informal advisory group of physicians and trustees and the Joint Conference Committee. This was marginally successful. Ultimately, there was no complete recovery from the missed opportunity for direct communication.

In most health services organizations, it may be difficult to find any stable coalition among physicians, governing boards, community groups, unions, affiliated institutions, and regulatory officials. The manager's primary political task in such situations may be to avoid being prominently identified with any particular power group. The manager will want to be seen by all groups as trustworthy and the most helpful contributor to the organization's effectiveness.

Political skills can be central to managerial success. Good politicians are always in touch with their public. They are good listeners and good communicators. This can be grueling and demanding work but each contact with a constituent can be educational as well as educating.

Suppose you are on good terms with many physicians, work long hours, do not encroach on the medical staff's territory, and meet the demands made on you by your superior or external agencies. Then why are you under political attack from individual physicians or the medical staff? What can go wrong for the hard-working, pleasant, attentive manager-politician?

There may be too many important physicians to please. Some physicians will not easily take no for an answer, nor will they tolerate indefinite delay. When physicians ask you for something that you cannot supply, obviously you should make sure that you really cannot get it for them. Although you do some things for certain physicians, you cannot always be as accommodating to all physicians. Preferential treatment may not be fair and will be resented, but organizations are not democracies and not all physicians contribute equally to the organization.

As a manager, you are often faced with the problem of "doing the right thing" (for the organization, for patients, for taxpayors) when physicians want to allocate scarce organizational resources in some way other than what you deem appropriate or acceptable. It is easier to deal with physician requests for expenditures that assist the organization financially but that do not help them personally than it is to address their personal desires. Do not attempt to start new services or recruit new physicians without cooperation from existing staff; new ventures, because they are new, are likely to be risky anyway.

On the other hand, nothing succeeds like success. Without risk, there is no gain. There is nothing quite like obtaining new resources for an organization or providing new services to patients, especially when predecessors and competitors have been unable to acquire or provide them.

Taking over an organization in political and financial shambles and restoring order to it can also demonstrate success. This turnaround is less difficult to accomplish if you set conditions before accepting the new position and reach out to key physicians and others who may reconsider past political conflict in the face of a worsening financial situation.

Organizational success should be shared. Physicians can help restore order when there has been political conflict and can advise the new manager on what should be done and how it can best be accomplished. Seek out the controversial and contributing physicians for ideas and the respected and elected physician officials for advice concerning implementation. Remember, however, that no one will be looking out for your political welfare.

Do not worry that physicians will be shy about telling you which obstacles to their work you should remove. In a hospital, removing obstacles may range from firing the director of nursing to increasing the size of the physicians' parking lot. When disaster strikes, you will usually have been given warning in the form of withdrawn contact, increased formality, or open hostility.

Your political capital can be spent in one shot if a physician hears from someone else something personal you have said about him or her. Political capital cannot be regained so quickly, and building political capital is a slow and tedious process; it is done day-by-day, hour-by-hour through your managerial persistence, discipline, expertise, and luck.

LIFE ON THE PHYSICIAN-DOMINATED COMMITTEE

An important part of the health services manager's job is serving on medical staff or hospital committees that are dominated by physicians.

Example: *Glory Hospital is part of a two-hospital system in an urban center. The two hospitals share a large number of physicians and are only five miles apart.* CEO *Phil Reddy established a strategic planning process with the medical staff to address the competition for Glory's core line of business, neuromuscular services.* CFO *John Kole staffed the task force charged with developing a business plan. Kole's group included a general surgeon as chair, a neurosurgeon from each hospital, an orthopedic surgeon from each hospital, a neurologist, a psychiatrist, and the product line manager. By the third meeting, Kole was at his wits' end. The physicians were calling each other names, refusing to attend any more meetings, and demanding that management get them more patients.*

Kole, recognizing the difficulty he was having, called for help. An outside consultant was retained to interview the committee members and develop recommendations as an outgrowth of those interviews.

The competitiveness between the physicians and the hospitals did not allow for reasonable conversation. The two neurosurgeons had previously argued and were not able to move past that point. Both were critical to any program expansion but not until they were able to see the benefit of working together. A third party with equivalent stature was needed to bring the two surgeons together.

Committees have become a necessary part of doing business in a hospital. They can be used to communicate, develop concepts, achieve concessions, or side-track plans any individual member dislikes. Thus, the structure and management of committee work must be addressed carefully and thoughtfully. The role of the manager on a physician committee is generally as staff to the committee; that is, she works with the chair to establish the agenda, assist in notifying members of meetings, do the scheduling, and take and prepare the minutes.

The clearer the focus of the committee and the more committed the chair, the easier it will be to build an agenda and produce results. In many cases, it is the manager's role to prepare and display data so that it provides useful and meaningful information.

The Joint Commission has mandated a number of functions for hospital boards and medical staffs that are handled in committees. Ad hoc committees are also established for everything from strategic planning to physician discipline.

The biggest risk for managers in physician committees is to play too dominant a role, unless asked to do so. Goal-oriented managers may scare physicians by driving toward an action before the other members are ready: think patience, long-term, collaboration, and buy-in.

MANAGING WITH NURSES

Example: *Benjamin Ringo, M.D., chair of pediatrics, complains to hospital CEO Victor Allen about the special care nursing staff. Allen asks Lydia Bailey, director of nursing, to respond. Ringo attacks hospital and nursing management for insensitivity to patient care management issues such as the training of nurses in a special unit, filling staff vacancies, and the lack of sufficient round-the-clock nursing coverage.*

Allen knows that the staffing in the medical ICU is right on the nationally recognized benchmarks, as measured either in hours per patient day or patient-to-staff ratios. He also knows that four positions had been filled with temporary agency nurses until this week. He asks Bailey to invite Ringo to participate in the orientation and training of the new staff. Allen also asks Bailey to undertake, with Ringo or one of his staff members, a process improvement initiative in the ICU aimed at customer satisfaction.

Nurses, the dominant workforce in many healthcare organizations, tend to be women who entered the profession to care for other people. In general, they are in an employee relationship with the organization. Their training can range from a two-year associate degree to a doctoral level. With some notable exceptions, few nurses have been exposed to formal managerial training during their academic work. Many organizations have developed alternative educational strategies to provide nurses with the managerial skills required to direct patient care services.

A nurse manager's job in a hospital is a challenging position. As the frontline manager, the nursing leader must balance demands from patients, patients' families, staff, physicians, and superiors. They are called on to make clinical decisions, mediate disagreements, and manage million-dollar organizations with grace and understanding. As economic pressures build on hospitals, the nurse manager is being asked to produce "patient care" more efficiently while keeping the customers—patients and physicians—enthusiastic about using the hospital.

Management's role is to support the first-line manager with skill training and timely and meaningful managerial tools (staffing benchmarks, financial reports, productivity reports, etc.).

CLINICIAN MANAGERS

As more clinicians are feeling the pressures of changing healthcare economics on their practices and see the opportunity to influence the future through management action, more are exploring managerial roles for themselves. According to C. Slater,[31] there are eight basic tasks for physician managers:

1. Determining or improving medical practices used in patient care;
2. Dealing with problems or differences between physicians;

3. Evaluating physician performance;
4. Advising and motivating physicians;
5. Recruiting physicians;
6. Improving the quality of patient care;
7. Dealing with external medical organizations; and
8. Improving professional knowledge and skills.

Nurse managers have similar responsibilities for nursing practice.

As more clinicians move into managerial roles, they will seek training and support. Your role will be to help guide the training of these fledgling managers. For the clinician, moving from a member of a peer group to a leadership role will stress their personal strengths and resolve.

Adapting Tom Peters' business prescription to healthcare, tomorrow's successful health services organization "will be a collection of skills and capabilities ever ready to respond to market opportunities."[32] Such skills and capabilities cannot be assumed to be satisfactorily in place as a consequence of an M.D., a B.S.N., or an M.B.A. degree received 15 years ago, or as a result of what managers, clinicians, or others have learned on the job. Instead, more educational programs should be planned and developed specific to organizational objectives and strategies, which are becoming increasingly measurable. What are the skills and experiences these managers need to lead an organization through the changes that will be required during the next three to five years and beyond? How can the organization ensure the development of these skills and capabilities?

We have raised some critical issues in working with the clinical staff in healthcare delivery organizations. A review of the offerings at several graduate management programs (NYU Wagner School and School of Nursing, University of Pennsylvania, Case Western Reserve University Weatherhead School) demonstrates the growing interest in managerial training for clinicians. The use of formal programs has both pros and cons that must be evaluated in terms of the individual's and institution's needs.

In recent years, the lines between chief operating officer and chief nursing officer (CNO) have blurred. CNOs with either formal managerial training or informal on-the-job training who demonstrate an interest in expanding their roles have developed into CEOs. The underlying clinical product of any healthcare organization makes a broad-thinking clinician a powerful resource and a compelling leader.

The same argument can be made for a physician who has the experience and inclination to become a manager. That individual can take on the leadership of a hospital, a group practice, or a health insurance company, or as senior vice president of medical affairs can influence physicians' in their strategic direction. The advantages are clear if the elements are there: a strong clinical understanding of the way the organization works and the products it is delivering, recognition by other clinicians of the training and experience the physician has, and a high regard for the physician by the nonmedical community.

The contrasting view is that few clinicians are interested in managerial roles, that managerial work is considered a necessary evil but it is not "real work." It is unusual for a physician, without the formal training, to have the interest in focusing on policy issues and strategic planning for an institution.

SUMMARY

We have discussed working with clinicians in a variety of situations. Organizations can be strengthened by the presence of solid clinical leadership working together with nonphysicians on management issues. The rate of change affecting all healthcare organizations will be successfully addressed only with a well-trained work force that can accept the changes and adapt. This includes sound clinical leadership.

Maxims for Healthcare Managers

> When you're talkin' you're not learnin'.
>
> — Ramsey Clark, former U.S. attorney general and civil rights
> and liberties advocate

ACCORDING TO KARL WEICK, "APHORISMS...can help people see facets of problems that they hadn't seen before. They can force people to keep asking questions, possibly improving the quality of questions that get asked. And they have the obvious advantage of honesty."[33] In the maxims that follow, we have borrowed freely from others and summed up some of what we have learned from the mistakes we have made as managers. The list is not meant to be exhaustive, but it does focus on some common and important problems that inexperienced—and not so inexperienced—managers create for themselves.

People are often rational when they disagree with you.

There is always a reason why something is being done the way it is. Before changing it, consider why it was done that way in the first place and who benefits from doing it that way. Next, consider what will happen to whom if things are done the way you are thinking of suggesting.

Beware of dividing people into "good guys" who agree with you and "bad guys" who disagree with you. For one thing, the bad guys are not a problem if they do not have powerful protectors or if you are not dependent on them and if you will not be working with them again in the future. Maybe the good guys don't really mean what they say in the sense that they will give you the necessary support you need after you stop talking with them and leave the room.

One approach to making changes is to present those whom the manager seeks to influence with the problem or challenge. Ask them to solve it. Then tell them what is right with their solutions.

Don't fear the vestedness of their interests; worry that you haven't done your homework.

Be prepared when someone asks, "How is your idea going to work?" You have to know better than anyone else how it is going to work, what might go wrong with it, and what the chances are that it will go wrong. Before implementing ideas that were successful elsewhere, be sure you have tailored them to fit your organization.

Worry about doing your homework rather than about physicians or others opposing you. If you have done your homework and others oppose you, at least you were not derelict in doing your job. If you have not done your homework, you should be discharged for wasting everybody's time—even if yours was a good idea that would have worked in the organization and people are only opposed to it because they have not worked out the details. Failure will be forgotten once and forgiven twice. The third time, look to your references and your resume.

If management doesn't make a difference, what are you doing anyway?

Respect your position, for without it, you would not have a job. Could the work you do be divided up and shared among other managers and nonmanagers? Does your work have to be done at all?

What are the most and the second most important aspects of your job? How well do you do them? Do you spend too much, just enough, or not enough time on the most important functions? Do people know what you are contributing? Do the key participants or stakeholders know? What new resources have you obtained for the organization lately?

Are you seen by the important stakeholders as helpful, even if not critical, to the organization? Do they see what you do as valuable or potentially valuable to them, or do they see you as a threat, a nullity, or an obstruction? You can make them perceive you as valuable by being cheerful, respectful, and considerate, and by consulting with them both before you make decisions that will affect them and after, during implementation. You want to be able to tell them in advance which of the promises you made that you may not be able to keep because of changed circumstances. All this consulting and negotiating takes considerable time, which means you will not be able to accomplish as much as you might like to. So what? No matter how much you accomplish, more remains to be done. You will benefit from investing in relationships with powerful people, and if you do your homework, making and implementing the next smart decision will take less time and go more smoothly.

Ask yourself what people want, not how you feel about them.

Assume that you have a fixed amount of time in which to deal with people whose work interacts with yours. When you spend time with certain people, you are choosing not to spend time with others. How are the others going to feel about your not spending enough time with them or too much time with somebody else?

There is an old saying: Managers should not get too close to their ballplayers. People compliment you, are pleasant to you, and use your time because they want something from you. There is nothing wrong with this; you are doing the same thing, otherwise you would not have gotten where you are.

It is not enough to remember that people will use you. How others perceive the people whom they think are using you may be just as important. Whatever you do with your favorites, even if you do not know they are favorites, will be interpreted by others to your disadvantage. Do people become your favorites by making significant contributions to organizational effectiveness, or do they get where they are primarily by flattery?

It is better to say no than maybe.

Always request a day in which to think about a new claim, demand, or request; never answer right away. If you say no, you can always reconsider, and the claimants will be grateful. If you say yes and then reconsider, the claimants will feel that you have taken something away from them and will bear a grudge.

Get your part of the bargain agreed to first; no bargaining is possible with people who are more powerful than you. Sometimes you cannot give people what they want because you do not have it to give—perhaps a third party, more powerful than you, is opposed. Always assume that if you give someone something he should not have, everyone else will know about it, and immediately.

If you aren't prepared when opportunity knocks, it may pass you by—or worse yet, you may grab it.

Plan for your next job now; that way, if someone asks you to take on more responsibility, you can begin thinking about the terms on which you would accept the offer.

The same thinking applies to accomplishment in your job. Stockpile ideas and plans so that when extra funds or time is available you will be prepared to move on them. It is never a waste of time to develop plans and strategies; the process helps you determine what is really possible for you to do now.

Consider how a proposed job change would affect your lifestyle and that of your family. Is your salary adequate now? What will the added stress and time at work entailed in a new job mean for you and your family?

Before accepting new responsibilities, know yourself and attempt to discover why you are being offered them. Is it because you have been effectively discharging your current responsibilities? If so, is there good reason to think that the new players and the rules of the new game will be similar? Do not move before you are ready, unless you are willing to risk failure. Most new managers have 40 to 45 years to work, so why rush to change a situation you were more or less happy with before you received the new offer?

If you aren't allowed to do what you want to do, focus on what you can do.

In any job there will decisions that you consider right and appropriate based on the long-range interests of the organization's clientele or the intentions of its founders, but that are not timely. Owners, trustees, and clinicians may perceive your contribution to the organizational welfare primarily in terms of your contribution to their own good, which may or may not coincide with what you consider to be the organizational welfare. But there is so much to be done to benefit patients and to support physicians, nurses, and others, why not get to work?

Do not blow your own trumpet too loudly or urge everyone else to make changes your way rather than their way. Results, not just working hard, are the desired contribution.

You should always have more to do than you can possibly accomplish. This does not always mean that you should do more work, only that you can always keep yourself fully occupied. There is joy in working well, but there is also joy in not having to rush everyone. Limit your time in the office; most managers are more dispensable at work than at home. Limit your thinking about work at home; it will make you a more interesting person. When you are working, however, focus your effort and concentrate on what is important. Be prepared to work extra hours, but only when appropriate.

Never say behind people's backs anything you wouldn't say to their faces.

There is a difference between speaking ill of what someone is doing and speaking ill of the person. If you are envious of or opposed to the person's policy, it is a sign of weakness to have to speak against the person in personal terms. Besides, the person to whom you are speaking may be the other person's friend or may agree with the other person's policy and not with yours.

There is an indirect way of speaking ill of others, which is by making statements about their personal lives that can only be interpreted as reflecting your value judgments. "Did you know that person X has been married three times, has a house in Shelter Island, has a son who is homosexual?," and so forth. Or, "Did you know person Y plays tennis Wednesday afternoons, eats at expensive restaurants at organizational expense, gives his secretary Thursday mornings off to see her psychiatrist?" Does telling someone else this kind of stuff do you any good, or are you spending valuable time worrying about what someone else is making or doing, what their friends are doing, how much they work, or whatever?

You should ask questions about other people or listen to what people say about others. You do need to know a lot about the people whose performance you depend on, but what you need to know is what they expect from you, how they perceive you, and what their strengths and limitations are. What people are saying about others can also be important because the speaker's feelings may affect work relationships. As a rule, however, you should counter negative comments about others with positive comments or validating questions such as, "Are you really sure?" "That isn't what I've observed about her," or "So what, he does a good job around here."

A related point is that you gain nothing by revealing yourself. Others will not necessarily reveal themselves if you do. Have respect for your position. School yourself to talk in pleasantries; even the weather can be really interesting if you are focusing on building a relationship rather than having a meaningful dialogue. When you reveal yourself you are defining yourself, and that gives somebody else a reason to dislike you. Further, you are showing favoritism to the person you tell. Maybe the someone else they tell your revelation to does not own something you own, or does not have kids as smart as your kids, and they resent it. What others do not know about you will not hurt you.

By the time you are really unhappy in your present job, you may not have adequate time for a job search.

Most managers do not stay with the same health services organization throughout their careers. Reasons for changing jobs include blocked advancement, the wish to try something new, a new boss with whom you do not want to work, and a new boss who is dissatisfied with your work.

You will probably begin to think of leaving your present job long before you are actually ready to do so, and you will probably stay at your present job for a while after you have decided that you are ready to move. Plan for moving well enough in advance to give yourself sufficient flexibility to respond to an appropriate opportunity and to accept largely on your own terms. Using a new offer to raise your current compensation is generally not wise. If your boss knows you are thinking of leaving, he or she may start thinking about replacing you.

You should be thinking frequently about what it is you want in a job, and you should be establishing and maintaining a network of acquaintances who can help you get where you want to be. At the same time, you must be producing results in your present position. Your boss's recommendation is always important. You can leave on friendly terms by having produced results and by not having asked the boss continually for something the boss could not give.

Establishing and maintaining a network of acquaintances can help you in your present job, and it should be enjoyable. "Doing favors" for other people includes listening to what they are saying, not just offering yourself through them to all potential employers. At the same time, you want some of your acquaintances to be people who can help you. There is not much you can do for well-established powerful people in return except be grateful, but that may be enough if you knew them before you were asking for a favor. If you strain to do something for someone of higher status, and the effort is inappropriate, it may not be appreciated. Seek out effective managers and seek the advice and assistance of experienced and respected mentors, some of whom may now be out of the mainstream of health services management. Their advice and judgment may be useful to you in deciding what to do, as well as in finding a specific job. Consider what they are telling you and let them know whether you intend to follow their advice. Let them know, too, how things turn out.

When people attack you, they aren't telling you everything.

If others attack you publicly, try not to respond immediately. Later ask them to tell you what is on their minds. What was behind what they are saying? Did they mean what you thought they meant? Were they responding to something they thought you said, and was that what you had intended to say? If not, say so. And you should not attack anyone more powerful than you openly or unexpectedly. Such an attack is sufficient reason for a boss to discharge you. If you are the boss, corporate life is difficult enough without having someone who is supposedly on your side be publicly disloyal.

Try to understand why certain people may dislike and fear you. Being disliked and feared is never going to do you any good unless you are top dog and powerful enough to remain so. You will be disliked if you are seen by powerful people as not being one of them by virtue of your occupation, age, sex, education, race, ethnic group, or whatever. Some people may think that you do not listen to them or appreciate them, that you play favorites, or that you do not take their views into account. They may find you inconsiderate, obtuse, depressing, or immoral. Do not give anyone an unnecessary reason for disliking you; the policies you advocate may be reason enough.

If others dislike your policies and wish to dislike you, they can find ample justification: you are too modest, formal, proper, cheerful for their tastes. These traits, however, may be what your position calls for and what others value in you. Uncommitted people in the organization are more likely to rally to your defense if they do not find your behavior threatening, unpredictable, or inappropriate.

Those who have helped you will help you again; as for those who have hurt you…

The amazing thing about human nature is not that there are so many brutish people but that there are so many kindly people. There may be no way for you to pay the kindly people back except by being kind to people who depend on you. When you ask people who have helped you once to help again, they generally do. What they have to give is not always what you want to receive, but their listening can help you refocus your thinking, plans, and action. Never surrender your judgment completely to anyone, but remember that you can further inform your judgment by responding genuinely to others' questions and concern.

When others speak ill of you, do not give you a chance, or oppose you on principle, your aim must be to ignore them, not to respond to them, not to ask them for anything, and not to expect anything from them. They are unlikely to tell you the real reasons they dislike or despise you; they are unlikely even to admit to you that they dislike or despise you. Being kind to those who have hurt you is only going to be interpreted as weakness or stupidity.

On the other hand, you will be the one who suffers if you seek revenge against those who have hurt you. It could breed more trouble, and, most importantly, feeling and expressing anger will distract you from the important work you have to do.

Don't expect from others what you aren't doing yourself.

Unrealistic expectations are as bad as overpromising. If you expect the impossible, it is only just that you be denied the possible. By all means, have high expectations of yourself. Work hard and well. The successful manager works harder and more intelligently than the competition. This attitude is what you want to encourage in those who work with you and for you.

Do not ask from others what you are unwilling to do, or haven't done, yourself. Of course, others do not have to do a job the same way you would do it—individuals have different strengths and weaknesses. It should not surprise you when your peers and subordinates do some of their tasks or perform some of their roles better than you can or do. This is as it should be, particularly when all of you share some of the same values, can appreciate each others' differences, and respect each others' talents and contributions.

10
Using the Computer:
Internet and E-mail

For a successful technology, reality must take precedence over public relations, for nature cannot be fooled.

— Richard P. Feynman, personal observations on the reliability of the space shuttle

IN THIS CHAPTER, WE WILL DISCUSS THE use of the computer as a tool that captures and dispenses information and through which the manager can direct the organization. We will not attempt to discuss the implications of the Internet and e-mail capabilities or the availability and reliability of information posted to the net.

JOB SEARCH

Example: *Susan Peters was invited to interview with the board of directors of a national professional organization for their* CEO *position. To be prepared for the interview, she searched for the organization on the Internet. She found their web site, including the history of the organization, its current work plans and initiatives, and a list of its current board officers and management.*

The Internet can be an adjunct to your search for employment. Having a basic knowledge of how to use search engines to cull out information is the first step. You will quickly discover a number of sites that list job openings and even assist in making your resume available to prospective employers. A health-related career site worth exploring is Health Care Source (www.healthcaresource.com).[34] A more generalized employment site is Career Mosaic (www.careermosaic.com) which allows you to search by type of position and by geography. As mentioned in Chapter 4, A C H E provides an online job bank and other career services for its members.

Several national employers and executive search organizations, such as Tyler and Company (www.tylerandco.com), now have web sites that list open positions. Large multi-site organizations, such as Columbia/H C A and Tenet, list a variety of job openings on their web sites. Resumes may be sent by e-mail and, with web browsers now available, the document does not have to be in A S C I I format but can be directly from a word processing program such as WordPerfect or Microsoft Word 97. It is still appropriate to follow up with a hard copy via the mail to ensure your personal information reaches its destination completely intact. Any job search contacts made via e-mail should be followed up by a more personal contact. Nothing is more important than establishing a personal relationship with the recruiter or hiring manager. The resume in whatever form — e-mail, fax, or hard copy — is only a piece of information that at best serves as an introduction. Thus, when contact is made via e-mail for a potential position, make sure the receiver gets a sense of the human being behind that resume.

J. Larry Tyler, president of Tyler and Company Executive Search, has a guide for job seekers, which includes a section on the use of the Internet. In his book, Mr. Tyler describes the ease of submitting a resume electronically. This form of submission allows the search firm to enter your personal information into their database with little significant effort. Many of the search firms are now requesting electronic submissions.[35]

Using the Internet as a source of information about the hiring organization can be quite valuable. At a minimum, web sites typically provide the organization's mission, a description of its services, and its location. Some organizations may include their annual report and a list of board members, along with other valuable information to enhance your interview. When looking at a new community, it is useful to visit the local chamber of commerce's web site or other local sources of information about the new community.

Exhibit 10.1

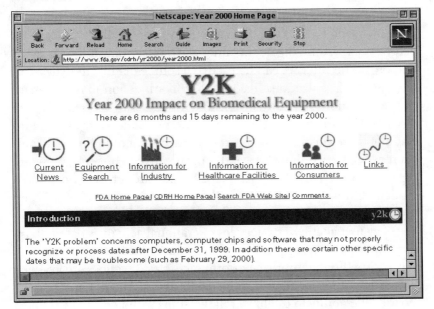

A MANAGEMENT TOOL

The new millennium created a new challenge for managers whose responsibilities include equipment that may not have been year 2000 compliant. As a source of information, the Internet can be invaluable for the manager.

Example: *Josie Janus, administrative director for clinical services at Northern Medical Center, served as the leader of the* Y2K *compliance team. Among her duties was to research equipment manufacturer's information about the* Y2K *compliance of their equipment. Rather than try to contact each vendor independently, Josie and her team begin to search vendor web sites for information about specific equipment and its compliance status. (See Exhibit 10.1.)*

Operating managers, planners, and financial officers can find the latest Medicare regulations posted within the Federal Register at the National Archives and Record Administration Web Site (http://www.access.gpo.gov/nara/index.html). The Joint Commission identifies its accreditation concerns and new standards on its web site (www.JCAHO. org). Professional organizations supporting healthcare practice have their own web pages, from the American College of Healthcare Executives (www.ACHE.org) to the American College of Cardiology (www. ACC.org). The Internet can be used as a source of current issues from accrediting organizations like the Joint Commission to national and state associations (i.e., the American Hospital Assosciation, www.AHA. org, and Healthcare Association of New York State, www.HANYS.org). Each of these sites provides current news pertinent to their missions, such as legislative initiatives and current survey concerns. Research organizations, such as Gallup and the Healthcare Advisory Board, have made their research available via the Internet using a universal document format based on software that is available free on the web.

A key management strategy for operational activity is based on understanding the best practices in the industry and using benchmarking as a method to improve performance. Best practices are available by participating in organizations such as the Healthcare Advisory Board. The ability to establish relationships with peers in other organizations and share information, techniques, and resources quickly and easily via the Internet and e-mail can facilitate the use of benchmarking strategies.

E-MAIL

As a tool to control your own organization, an intranet e-mail system can be quite powerful. It can distribute daily, weekly, and monthly management reports. With the ability to move data between various databases, managers can design their own monitoring systems and tools, or the organization can develop templates for specific reporting requirements.

Example: *Coastal Healthcare Partnership was struggling to keep its costs in line as its admissions fluctuated from week to week. Stuart Johns, the C F O, designed a spreadsheet-based monitoring template for the first-line managers to use on a monthly basis. He e-mailed it to each of them with detailed instructions. The department managers downloaded the templates with all the calculations built in. The managers merely had to enter their specific data. The results were then e-mailed back to Johns*

Exhibit 10.2

	Exhibit 10.2					
Coastal Healthcare Partnership						
Run Rate vs '99 Budget				Positive Variance - doing well		
				Negative Variance - needs work		
Hospital:	Coastal					
Cost Center #	555					
Cost Center Name:	Your Department Here					
					Monthly Avg	
				Oct-Nov	1st Qtr	
				Average	Budget '99	Variance	Var%
Statistic						
Stat Name (UOS):						
Stat Name Here	aaa	bbb	"=(H16+G16)/2	rrr	"=(G16=H16)/2-K16	"=M16/K16
Manhours/UOS	ccc	ddd	"=(H16+G18)/2	sss	"=K18-(G18+H18)/2	"=M18/K18
Supply $ / UOS	"=G30/G16	"H30/H16	"=(H20+G20)/2	"=K30/K16	"K20-(G20+H20)/2	"=M20/K20
Expenses						
Salaries, Wages & Benefits...	eee	fff	"=(H26+G26)/2	ttt	"=K26-J26	"=M26/K26
Contract Labor...	qqq	hhh	"=(H28+G28)/2	uuu	"=K28-J28	"=M28/K28
Supplies	iii	jjj	"=(H30+G30)/2	vvv	"=K30-J30	"=M30/K30
Action Plan						
Enter Text here...						

Sheet1 / Sheet2 / Sheet3

and the COO *for review. The immediate effect was a 5-percent reduction in supply costs and a 7-percent reduction in hours worked. (See Exhibit 10.2.)*

E-mail as a communications tool is both a boon and a bust. It enables the user to share information with one or a great many people at the same time. This makes sending broad messages via the Internet, or intranet in the case of "wired organizations," very easy. In many cases, communication is enhanced. E-mail can be used as a way to avoid "telephone tag" and keep the manager's constituency informed about issues affecting the entire organization. In the authors' organizations, all managers and most other staff have access to e-mail. Thus, broad-based announcements, as well as individual communications, can be handled efficiently.

E-mail has made group work more productive. On the other hand, there is a tremendous amount of superfluous material being distributed just because it is easy. Add a group of names to a distribution list and off you go. Our recent experience has suggested that a considerable amount of what gets shared may not be worth sharing and gets deleted by the receiving party without being read. This author has found that e-mail can be a time saver for keeping other staff informed and up-to-date. It simplifies short communications and messages that require wide distribution. With e-mail connected all the time, a quick note is easy to send and receive. Larger messages and attachments are not easily dealt with on the screen. A survey of middle managers suggested that the longer the message, the more likely it will be ignored or saved until it can be printed and reviewed without distraction. When writing this text, the authors often used e-mail to discuss the status of their work and comment on changes.

Sending multiple copies of an e-mail enables many people to stay informed. However, if the originator is not clear when asking for an action or a response, she may get a conflicting outcome. Thus, as in most communications, you must be clear about whom you are addressing and what you are directing them to do.

A useful resource and guide for the beginning healthcare Internet user is a free publication by The Robert Wood Johnson Foundation, *The RWJF Internet Handbook: Basic, Specialized, Health Care and Grant Seeking Resources on the World Wide Web*, May 1998, by Michelle M. Volesko.

Example: *Nan Klyne*, R.N., *manages the Quality Improvement Program at North Coast Community Hospital. She has recently completed her master's program in healthcare management. As a result of her schedule and access to several libraries via the Internet, she can complete her research when it suits her schedule. To keep up with her professional interests, Nan uses several listserves for quality improvement, case management, and geriatric care. (See Exhibit 10.3.)*

Extensive use of these new communications tools has given managers access to peers and colleagues around the world with the ease of using a keyboard. We find professionals engaged in group projects and sharing policies, educational programs, ideas, and resumes. The tools of the Internet, e-mail, web sites, listserves, and chat rooms have extended an individual's knowledge base and influence exponentially.

Exhibit 10.3

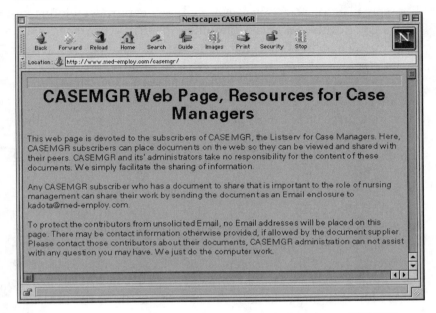

Note: Reprinted with permission from Al Todak of Medical Employment Services and owner of CASE MGR.

CONSUMER USE OF THE INTERNET

With information only a click away, your customers are becoming as knowledgeable as you are about their diseases and the alternative therapies. They are also becoming increasingly knowledgeable about the quality of your organization and your physicians. The University of Iowa College of Medicine maintains a Virtual Hospital, and provides consumers with detailed information about using the Iowa Health Sciences Center, about its physicians, and about many diseases (www. vh.org). Columbia Presbyterian Hospital in New York (now New York Presbyterian Hospital) maintains a large disease-specific database in the form of a *Complete Home Medical Guide* (cpmcnet.cpmc. columbia.edu/texts/guide/all.html), as do many hospitals, insurance carriers, and managed care companies.

The *New York Times*[36] has reported that more employers are pushing decisions about healthcare services to their employees. They are doing this by offering access to the Internet and, specifically, to several web sites, including HealthPages (www.thehealthpages.com), which lists more than 500,000 physicians as well as other provider information and directories; the National Committee on Quality Assurance (www. ncqa.org), which tracks accreditation status and quality levels at most major HMOs; and the HealthFinder (healthfinder.gov), where the Federal government furnishes information on how to chose quality healthcare services.

With a little effort, consumers of your services can research their symptoms, determine if your organization has a good track record with the disease in question, and identify which physicians are skilled at treating the problem.

Because it is relatively easy to develop a web site and post information, what the consumer gets may not be accurate and often needs to be explained by a knowledgeable professional. There will be more questions and more questioning of outcomes, credentials, efficacy, and alternatives. Thus, the potential is there to enhance all aspects of performance and care for your patients.

As with most sources of data, the challenge for the user will be how to separate useful information from everything else that is put forth.

11

Professional Organizations for Health Services Managers

AN UP-AND-COMING MANAGER IN A HEALTH services organization is immediately challenged by the numerous and rapidly changing financial and operational demands that face the healthcare industry.

To be effective, managers must establish themselves as full participants in the institution's decision-making process and culture. Success in a new environment is often associated with the extent to which managers familiarize themselves with the operations of the organization and contribute to its activities.

However, focusing on operations exclusively can sometimes become an all-consuming task for the developing manager, whose role in the institution may become more and more insular. To maintain enthusiasm and serve as a source of new and creative ideas, it may be necessary to get outside encouragement. The up-and-coming manager should be involved in professional associations that offer opportunities to network, develop a sense of alternate modes of action, and stay current on global and external issues.

Professional organizations provide the following important services to administrators:

- more objective perspective of common elements in healthcare institutions;
- current information on new issues and technology;
- research;
- opportunity to engage in discussions on topics of specific interest;
- continuing education and training for ongoing professional growth;
- development of professional standards;
- participation in advocacy and shaping policy issues on the local or national level;
- a lobbying group to protect the interests of members; and
- service to the community.

A range of national and regional professional organizations are available for managers to participate in, with specific interests from administration and graduate medical education to long-term care. Examples of some of the more prominent and active national associations by type of institution include the following.

Hospitals/Other Health Services

The American College of Healthcare Executives (ACHE) (www.ACHE. org) is an international professional society of nearly 30,000 healthcare executives. With comprehensive programs in credentialing, education, career counseling, publications, research, and public policy, ACHE works toward its goal of improving the health status of society by advancing healthcare management excellence.

Hospitals

American Hospital Association (AHA) (www.AHA.org) in Chicago was founded in 1899. The mission of the AHA is to advance the health of individuals and communities. The AHA leads, represents, and serves healthcare provider organizations that are accountable to the community and committed to health improvement. The AHA serves all types of hospitals, healthcare networks, and their patients and communities.

Close to 5,000 institutional, 600 associate, and 40,000 personal members form the AHA.

Long-term Care Facilities

American College of Health Care Administrators (ACHCA) (www. ACHCA.org) in Alexandria, Virginia, was founded in 1962 and is the professional society for nearly 6,300 administrators in long-term care, assisted living, and subacute care. Its mission is to be the premier organization serving as a catalyst to empower administrators who will define professionalism throughout the continuum of care.

Academic Medical Centers

Association of American Medical Colleges (AAMC) (www.aamc.org), founded 1876, is a nonprofit association comprising the 125 accredited U.S. medical schools; the 16 accredited Canadian medical schools; more than 400 major teaching hospitals and health systems, including 70 Department of Veterans Affairs medical centers; nearly 90 academic and professional societies representing 75,000 faculty members; and the nation's medical students and residents.

As an association of medical schools, teaching hospitals, and academic societies, the AAMC has as its purpose the improvement of the nation's health through the advancement of academic medicine. The AAMC services include legislative and regulatory monitoring of federal health initiatives in the areas of hospital and physician payment, biomedical research, technology, medical education, and physician work force issues; representation and testimony at key congressional hearings; access to the Association's numerous databases; and staff support in the interpretation and analysis of national policy issues.

The Council of Teaching Hospitals of the Association of American Medical Colleges (COTH/AAMC) (http://www.aamc.org/about/ coth/start.htm) in Washington, D.C., was founded in 1965. The Council's mission is to provide representation and services related to the special needs, concerns, and opportunities facing major teaching hospitals in the United States and Canada. The Council is the principal source of hospital and health system input into overall Association

policy and direction. Although approximately 1,100 hospitals are involved in graduate medical education in this country, the 400 COTH
member institutions train about three-quarters of the residents in the
United States. COTH members receive the full range of AAMC and
Council-specific services.

Group Practices

Medical Group Management Association (MGMA) (www.MGMA.com)
in Engelwood, Colorado, was founded in 1926. The MGMA is the leading organization representing medical group practice nationwide.
About 8,300 healthcare organizations and 21,000 individuals are MGMA
members, representing more than 209,000 physicians. The organization's core purpose is to improve the effectiveness of medical group
practices and the knowledge and skills of the individuals who manage
and lead them.

HMOs

American Association of Health Plans, formerly Group Health Association of America (GHAA) (www.AAHP.org) was founded in 1996 and
is located in Washington, D.C. The AAHP represents more than 1,000
HMOs, PPOs, and other network-based plans. The AAHP's member
companies are dedicated to a philosophy of healthcare that puts the
patient first; together these companies care for close to 140 million
Americans.

Public Health

American Public Health Association (APHA) (www.APHA.org) in Washington, D.C., founded in 1872, is the oldest and largest organization of
public health professionals in the world, representing more than 50,000
members from more than 50 occupations of public health. The APHA
is concerned with a broad set of issues affecting personal and environmental health, including federal and state funding for health programs,
pollution control, programs and policies related to chronic and infec-
tious diseases, a smoke-free society, and professional education in public health.

Minority Health

National Association of Health Services Executives (NAHSE) (www.
NAHSE.org) in Washington, D.C., is a nonprofit association of black
healthcare executives founded in 1968 to promote the advancement
and development of black healthcare leaders and elevating the quality of healthcare services rendered to minority and underserved communities. NAHSE has sponsored and participated in local and national
programs and projects designed to improve quality, access, and availability to health services and to expand educational opportunities in
the field of health services administration. NAHSE's purpose is to ensure greater participation of minority groups in the health field. Its
basic objective is to develop and maintain a strong viable national
body to more effectively influence the national healthcare delivery
system. It has provided a vehicle for blacks to effectively participate in
the design, direction, and delivery of quality healthcare to all people.

Women

Women in Health Care Management (WHCM) (www.WHCM.org) provides a forum for professional women to network, share information,
meet their peers, and keep abreast of developments in the field. Members of WHCM work in all healthcare settings, from acute care hospitals to HMOs, consulting firms, private nonprofits, and long-term care
facilities. They work at many levels, from junior supervisory positions
to senior management roles. WHCM offers its members a variety of
valuable services, including quarterly networking meetings, two large
annual meetings, inclusion in a member directory, a quarterly news-
letter, small group sessions, a job bank, and mentoring.

Financial Management

Healthcare Financial Management Association (www.hfma.org) in
Westchester, Illinois, founded in 1946, is the nation's leading personal
membership organization for more than 35,000 financial management
professionals employed by hospitals, integrated delivery systems, long-
term and ambulatory care facilities, managed care organizations, medical group practices, public accounting and consulting firms, insurance

companies, government agencies, and other healthcare organizations. The HFMA, through its chapters, regions, and national office, helps members meet challenges by providing professional development opportunities, influencing healthcare policy, and communicating information and technical data.

Information Systems

Healthcare Information Management Systems Society (HIMSS) (www. himss.org) is a nonprofit organization representing information and management systems professionals in healthcare, serving its members, its customers, and the industry by providing leadership, education, and networking. The HIMSS represents more than 12,000 individual leaders in four professional areas: clinical systems, information systems, management engineering, and telecommunications. Members are responsible for developing many of today's key innovations in healthcare delivery and administration, including telemedicine, computer-based patient records, community health information networks, and portable/wireless healthcare computing.

Quality Assurance

The National Committee for Quality Assurance (www.ncqa.org) is a private, nonprofit organization dedicated to assessing and reporting on the quality of managed care plans. It is governed by a board of directors that includes employers, consumer and labor representatives, health plans, quality experts, policymakers, and representatives from organized medicine. The NCQA's mission is to provide information that enables purchasers and consumers of managed healthcare to distinguish among plans based on quality, thereby allowing them to make more informed healthcare purchasing decisions. This will encourage plans to compete based on quality and value, rather than on price and provider network alone. The NCQA's efforts are organized around two activities, accreditation and performance measurement, which are complementary strategies for producing information to guide choice.

Descriptions of all the above organizations were taken from organizational publications, membership information, and web sites.

Appendix A: Chief Executive Officer Employment Agreement

THIS AGREEMENT, MADE AND EFFECTIVE AS of the 1st day of July, 1991, between Wilkins Hospital, hereinafter referred to as the Hospital, and Max Griffin, hereinafter referred to as Mr. Griffin.

Whereas, the Hospital desires to continue the service of Mr. Griffin for three (3) years from the effective date of this agreement and Mr. Griffin desires to accept such employment.

Now, therefore, in consideration of the material advantages accruing to the parties and the mutual covenants contained herein, the Hospital and Mr. Griffin agree with each other as follows:

1. *Responsibilities*—Mr. Griffin will render full-time professional services to the Hospital in the capacity of President and Chief Executive Officer of the Hospital for the three (3)-year term of this contract. He will at all times, faithfully, industriously, and to the best of his ability, perform all duties that may be required of him by virtue of his position as Chief Executive Officer and all duties set forth in the Hospital bylaws to the reasonable satisfaction of and in appropriate consultation with the Hospital Board. His duties shall specifically include, but not necessarily be limited to, the following, to wit:
   A. He will perfect and submit to the Board of Directors for approval a schematic organization of the personnel concerned with the operation of the Hospital.
   B. He will develop a strategic plan that is consistent with the Hospital's mission and will develop and carry out annual operating plans necessary to achieve organizational objectives.
   C. He will select, employ, control, and have authority to discharge any Hospital employee or other individuals serving in positions that might otherwise be occupied by employees. Employment shall be subject to budget authorization granted by the Board.

D. He will supervise providers of professional service (i.e., legal and accounting) and make recommendations to the Board of Trustees concerning their engagement.

E. He will be a voting member of the Hospital Board and will report to the Hospital Board, at regular and special meetings, all significant items of business of the Hospital and make recommendatins concerning the disposition thereof.

F. He will submit regularly, in cooperation with the appropriate committee of the Hospital Board of Trustees and the Chair, periodic reports showing the professional services rendered and the financial activities of the Hospital.

G. He will prepare annual operating and capital budgets for Board approval as well as a three (3)-year capital expenditure plan. Within this context, he will make recommendations concerning the purchase of supplies and equipment and service by the Hospital and will cause to be established a system for planning and approving such expenditures.

H. He will attend all meetings of the Board of Trustees and he may attend meetings of the various committees of the Board.

I. He will serve as a liaison between the Hospital Board and the medical staff of the Hospital with full responsibility for the operation of the Hospital. He will cooperate with the medical staff and secure like cooperation on the part of all concerned with rendering professional service to the end that the patients may receive the best possible care.

J. He will be the official spokesperson for the Hospital with emphasis on community outreach and securing of various forms of support.

K. He will keep abreast and be informed of new developments in the medical and administrative areas of Hospital administration.

L. He will oversee the physical plant, Hospital building, and grounds, and keep them in good state of repair, conferring with the appropriate committee of the Hospital Board of Trustees in major matters, but carrying out routine repairs and maintenance without such consultation.

M. He will supervise all business affairs such as the records of financial transactions, collection of accounts and purchase and issuance of supplies, and be certain that all funds are collected and expended to the best possible advantage.

N. He will supervise the preservation of the permanent medical records of the Hospital and act as overall custodian of those records.

2. *Compensation*

A. In consideration for these services as Chief Executive Officer, Wilkins Hospital agrees to pay the sum of $200,000 per annum, payable in twelve (12) equal monthly installments, or such higher figure as shall be agreed upon at an annual review of his compensation by the Board. Mr. Griffin may, at his option, require such portion of said salary as he may designate be put into tax-sheltered investments as deferred income, subject to applicable laws.

B. In addition to the $200,000 per year base salary, Mr. Griffin shall be eligible to receive additional incentive compensation as follows:

i. Up to $30,000 related to his first twelve (12) months of employment as the result of achieving financial performance targets based on the 1991 and 1992 budgets and the cash flow projections which are Exhibit B, dated May 14, 1991. Each of these six goals will have a value of $5,000. The Hospital may award Mr. Griffin a portion of the incentive payment if a goal has been substantially achieved and the Hospital's performance has resultantly improved. In the event there is a reasonable basis to question whether one or more goals has been met, the decision of the Hospital's Board of Trustees in that regard shall be conclusive and binding.

a. December 31, 1991, Year End Results (based on 1991 audit)
   - Gain/Loss from Operations
     $500,000
   - Excess of Expenses over Revenues
     $1,500,000
   - Cash on Hand
     $1,000,000

b. June 30, 1992 (six months of budget year 1992)
   - Gain/Loss from Operations
     $750,000
   - Excess of Expenses over Revenues
     $1,850,000
   - Cash on Hand
     $2,300,000

The 1991 goals are based on exceeding the revised 1991 budget projections. The specific figures on which Mr. Griffin's 1992 performance will be evaluated will be based on the Board approved 1992 budget.

ii. Up to $20,000 related to his first twelve (12) months of employment as the result of achieving other operational and planning goals important to the Hospital's future. These goals are to become a part of this agreement no later than July 1, 1991.

a. Mr. Griffin's performance will be evaluated semi-annually by the Board of Trustees and his salary will be reviewed annually. Decision regarding incentive compensation will be made semi-annually with the first such review occurring in early 1992 based on personal and organizational performance during the period July 1–December 31, 1992.

b. Based on Mr. Griffin's performance and market conditions, the Hospital shall endeavor to maintain his compensation and benefits at a level commensurate with his peers in the healthcare industry and the rate of general influation in the economy. In addition, during the period of this agreement, Mr. Griffin shall continue to be eligible for incentive payments which each year shall have a minimum potential value of at least as much as those provided for in the first year of this agreement ($50,000).

3. *Benefits*

A. Mr. Griffin shall be entitled to accrue sick leave at the rate of 12 days per year up to a maximum of 60 days in accordance with Hospital policy for management and professional personnel.

B. Mr. Griffin will earn 20 vacation days per year as per the Hospital policy. He will also be entitled to eight paid holidays plus four personal days per year in accordance with Hospital policy.

C. In addition, Mr. Griffin will be permitted to be absent from the Hospital during working days to attend professional meetings and to attend to such outside professional duties in the hospital field as have been mutually agreed upon between him and the Chair of the Board. Attendance at such approved meetings and accomplishment of approved professional duties shall be fully compensated service time and shall not be considered vacation time. The Hospital shall reimburse Mr. Griffin for all reasonable expenses incurred by him incident to attendance at approved professional meetings and such reasonable entertainment expenses incurred by Mr. Griffin in furtherance of the Hospital's interests, provided, however, that such reimbursement is appropriate and within the limits of the Hospital budget.

D. Nothing contained herein shall prohibit Mr. Griffin from maintaining membership in or participating in private, social, or civic endeavors that do not interfere with or detract from his performance of this agreement.

E. The Hospital agrees to pay dues to professional associations and societies and to such service organizations and clubs of which Mr.

Griffin is a member, approved by the Chair of the Board as being in the best interest of the Hospital.

F. In the event of a single period of prolonged inability to work because of the results of a sickness or an injury, Mr. Griffin will be compensated at his full rate of pay for a period of six (6) months from the date of such sickness or injury, provided, however, that the compensation shall be reduced by any disability income paid to Mr. Griffin pursuant to any disability policy in effect under this agreement.

4. *Additional benefits*—Subject to applicable tax laws and regulations, the Hospital will also at its expense

   A. insure Mr. Griffin under its Directors and Officers liability insurance policy for all acts done by him in good faith as Chief Executive Officer throughout the term of this agreement;

   B. provide, throughout the term of this contract, a term life insurance policy for Mr. Griffin in an amount equivalent to two times his annual salary, payable to the beneficiary of his choice;

   C. provide the Hospital's standard comprehensive health and major medical insurance for Mr. Griffin and his eligible dependents;

   D. provide an annual executive physician examination;

   E. furnish an automobile for Mr. Griffin's full-time use, including expenses related to its use;

   F. contribute on behalf of Mr. Griffin to the Hospital's standard pension plan;

   G. provide standard "key person" long-term disability income protection plan.

5. *Termination*

   A. The Board may, in its discretion, terminate Mr. Griffin's duties as Chief Executive Officer. Such action shall require a vote of the Board and become effective when such vote is taken. After such termination, all rights, duties, and obligations of both parties shall cease except that the Hospital shall continue to pay Mr. Griffin his then monthly salary for the month in which his duties were terminated and for twelve (12) consecutive months thereafter. During this period, Mr. Griffin shall not be required to perform any duties for the Hospital or come to the Hospital. Neither shall the fact that he seeks, accepts, and undertakes other employment during this period affect such payments. Also, for the period during which such payments are being made, the Hospital agrees to keep Mr. Griffin's life insurance, disability income protection, and major medical insurance coverage paid up and in effect.

   B. In the event Mr. Griffin is charged by proper State or Federal authority with the commission of a felony, Mr. Griffin may be immediately suspended, with or without pay at Board discretion, until final disposition of the charge. Upon conviction, the Board may terminate the agreement in its entirety, in which case the Board is free from all objections hereunder. In the event such charges result in an acquittal, Mr. Griffin shall be restored to his position with all back pay and this agreement shall remain in full force and effect.

6. Should the Board in its discretion change Mr. Griffin's duties so it can reasonably be found that he is no longer performing the duties of the Chief Executive Officer of the Hospital, Mr. Griffin shall have the right, in his complete discretion, to terminate this contract by written notice delivered to the Chair of the Board. After such termination, all rights, duties, and obligations of both shall cease except that the Hospital shall continue to pay Mr. Griffin his then monthly salary for the month in which his duties were terminated and for twelve (12) consecutive months thereafter. During this period Mr. Griffin shall not be required to perform any duties of the Hospital or come to the Hospital. Neither shall the fact that he seeks, accepts, or undertakes other employment during this term affect such payments. Also, for the period during which such payments are being made, the Hospital agrees to keep Mr. Griffin's life insurance, disability income protection, and medical insurance paid up and in effect.

7. Should Mr. Griffin in his discretion elect to terminate this contract for any other reason than as stated in paragraphs 5 or 6, he shall give the Board four (4) months' written notice of his decision to terminate. During such four (4) months' notice period, Mr. Griffin will be expected to perform his duties in accordance with this agreement. At the end of these four (4) months, all rights, duties, and obligations of both parties to the contract shall cease.

8. Negotiations for the extension of this contract, or for agreement on the terms of a new contract, shall be completed, or the decision not to negotiate a new contract made, not later than the end of the seventh month of the final contract year. By mutual agreement of the parties, this contract and all its terms and conditions may be extended from year to year or for a term beyond its initial term by a simple letter exchanged between the parties at any time during the contract term. In the event Mr. Griffin elects not to renew this agreement he shall be bound by the notice and performance provisions of paragraph 7 of this agreement. In the event the Hospital elects not to renew this agreement it shall be bound by the notice, payment, and other provisions of paragraph 5a of this agreement.

9. This contract constitutes the entire agreement between the parties and contains all the agreements between them with respect to the subject matter hereof. It also supersedes any and all other agreements or contracts,

either oral or written, between the parties with respect to the subject matter hereof.

10. Except as otherwise specifically provided, the terms and conditions of this contract may be amended at any time by mutual agreement of the parties, provided that before any amendment shall be valid or effective it shall have been reduced to writing and signed by the Chair of the Board and Mr. Griffin.

11. The invalidity or unenforceability of any particular provision of this contract shall not affect its other provisions, and this contract shall be construed in all respects as if such invalid or unenforceable provision had been omitted unless such omission substantially impairs the benefit of this agreement for either party.

12. This agreement shall be binding upon and inured to the benefit of the Hospital, its successor and assigns, and shall be binding upon Mr. Griffin, his administrator, executors, legatees, heirs, and assigns.

Appendix B: American College of Healthcare Executives *Code of Ethics*^{*1}

PREFACE

The *Code of Ethics* is administered by the Ethics Committee, which is appointed by the Board of Governors upon nomination by the Chairman. It is composed of at least nine Fellows of the College, each of whom serves a three-year term on a staggered basis, with three members retiring each year.

The Ethics Committee shall:

- Review and evaluate annually the *Code of Ethics*, and make any necessary recommendations for updating the *Code*.
- Review and recommend action to the Board of Governors on allegations brought forth regarding breaches of the *Code of Ethics*.
- Develop ethical policy statements to serve as guidelines of ethical conduct for healthcare executives and their professional relationships.
- Prepare an annual report of observations, accomplishments, and recommendations to the Board of Governors, and such other periodic reports as required.

The Ethics Committee invokes the *Code of Ethics* under authority of the ACHE *Bylaws*, Article II, Membership, Section 6, Resignation and Termination of Membership; Transfer to Inactive Status, subsection (b), as follows:

Membership may be terminated or rendered inactive by action of the Board of Governors as a result of violation of the Code of Ethics; *nonconformity with the* Bylaws *or* Regulations Governing Admission, Advancement, Recertification, and Reappointment;

---

*As amended by the Council of Regents at its annual meeting on August 22, 1995.

¹Appendices I and II, entitled "American College of Healthcare Executives Grievance Procedure" and "Ethics Committee Action," respectively, are a material part of the *Code of Ethics* and are incorporated herein by reference.

Reprinted with permission of the American College of Healthcare Executives.

conviction of a felony; or conviction of a crime of moral turpitude or a crime relating to the healthcare management profession. No such termination of membership or imposition of inactive status shall be effected without affording a reasonable opportunity for the member to consider the charges and to appear in his or her own defense before the Board of Governors or its designated hearing committee, as outlined in the "Grievance Procedure," Appendix I of the College's Code of Ethics.

PREAMBLE

The purpose of the *Code of Ethics* of the American College of Healthcare Executives is to serve as a guide to conduct for members. It contains standards of ethical behavior for healthcare executives in their professional relationships. These relationships include members of the healthcare executive's organization and other organizations. Also included are patients or others served, colleagues, the community, and society as a whole. The *Code of Ethics* also incorporates standards of ethical behavior governing personal behavior, particularly when that conduct directly relates to the role and identity of the healthcare executive.

The fundamental objectives of the healthcare management profession are to enhance overall quality of life, dignity, and well-being of every individual needing healthcare services; and to create a more equitable, accessible, effective, and efficient healthcare system.

Healthcare executives have an obligation to act in ways that will merit the trust, confidence, and respect of healthcare professionals and the general public. Therefore, healthcare executives should lead lives that embody an exemplary system of values and ethics.

In fulfilling their commitments and obligations to patients or others served, healthcare executives function as moral advocates. Since every management decision affects the health and well-being of both individuals and communities, healthcare executives must carefully evaluate the possible outcomes of their decisions. In organizations that deliver healthcare services, they must work to safeguard and foster the rights, interests, and prerogatives of patients or others served. The role of moral advocate requires that healthcare executives speak out and take actions necessary to promote such rights, interests, and prerogatives if they are threatened.

I. The Healthcare Executive's Responsibilities to the Profession of Healthcare Management
    The healthcare executive shall:
    A. Uphold the values, ethics and mission of the healthcare management profession;
    B. Conduct all personal and professional activities with honesty, integrity, respect, fairness, and good faith in a manner that will reflect well upon the profession;

c. Comply with all laws pertaining to healthcare management in the jurisdictions in which the healthcare executive is located, or conducts professional activities;

D. Maintain competence and proficiency in healthcare management by implementing a personal program of assessment and continuing professional education;

E. Avoid the exploitation of professional relationships for personal gain;

F. Use this *Code* to further the interests of the profession and not for selfish reasons;

G. Respect professional confidences;

H. Enhance the dignity and image of the healthcare management profession through positive public information programs; and

I. Refrain from participating in any activity that demeans the credibility and dignity of the healthcare management profession.

II. The Healthcare Executive's Responsibilities to Patients or Others Served, to the Organization, and to Employees

A. Responsibilities to Patients or Others Served
The healthcare executive shall, within the scope of his or her authority:

1. Work to ensure the existence of a process to evaluate the quality of care or service rendered;

2. Avoid practicing or facilitating discrimination and institute safeguards to prevent discriminatory organizational practices;

3. Work to ensure the existence of a process that will advise patients or others served of the rights, opportunities, responsibilities, and risks regarding available healthcare services;

4. Work to provide a process that ensures the autonomy and self-determination of patients or others served; and

5. Work to ensure the existence of procedures that will safeguard the confidentiality and privacy of patients or others served.

B. Responsibilities to the Organization
The healthcare executive shall, within the scope of his or her authority:

1. Provide healthcare services consistent with available resources and work to ensure the existence of a resource allocation process that considers ethical ramifications;

2. Conduct both competitive and cooperative activities in ways that improve community healthcare services;

3. Lead the organization in the use and improvement of standards of management and sound business practices;

4. Respect the customs and practices of patients or others served, consistent with the organization's philosophy; and

5. Be truthful in all forms of professional and organizational communication, and avoid disseminating information that is false, misleading, or deceptive.

C. Responsibilities to Employees

Healthcare executives have an ethical and professional obligation to employees of the organizations they manage that encompass but are not limited to:

1. Working to create a working environment conducive for underscoring employee ethical conduct and behavior;

2. Working to ensure that individuals may freely express ethical concerns and providing mechanisms for discussing and addressing such concerns;

3. Working to ensure a working environment that is free from harrassment, sexual and other; coercion of any kind, especially to perform illegal or unethical acts; and discrimination on the basis of race, creed, color, sex, ethnic origin, age, or disability;

4. Working to ensure a working environment that is conducive to proper utilization of employees' skills and abilities;

5. Paying particular attention to the employee's work environment and job safety; and

6. Working to establish appropriate grievance and appeals mechanisms.

III. Conflicts of Interest

A conflict of interest may be only a matter of degree, but exists when the healthcare executive:

A. Acts to benefit directly or indirectly by using authority or inside information, or allows a friend, relative, or associate to benefit from such authority or information; or

B. Uses authority or information to make a decision to intentionally affect the organization in an adverse manner.

The healthcare executive shall:

A. Conduct all personal and professional relationships in such a way that all those affected are assured that management decisions are made in the best interests of the organization and the individuals served by it;

B. Disclose to the appropriate authority any direct or indirect financial or personal interests that pose potential or actual conflicts of interest;

C. Accept no gifts or benefits offered with the express or implied expectation of influencing a management decision; and

D. Inform the appropriate authority and other involved parties of potential or actual conflicts of interest related to appointments or elections to boards or committees inside or outside the healthcare executive's organization.

IV. The Healthcare Executive's Responsibilities to Community and Society

The healthcare executive shall:

A. Work to identify and meet the healthcare needs of the community;

B. Work to ensure that all people have reasonable access to healthcare services;

C. Participate in public dialogue on healthcare policy issues and advocate solutions that will improve health status and promote quality healthcare;

D. Consider the short-term and long-term impact of management decisions on both the community and on society; and

E. Provide prospective consumers with adequate and accurate information, enabling them to make enlightened judgments and decisions regarding services.

V. The Healthcare Executive's Responsibility to Report Violations of the *Code*

A member of the College who has reasonable grounds to believe that another member has violated this *Code* has a duty to communicate such facts to the Ethics Committee.

APPENDIX I

American College of Healthcare Executives Grievance Procedure

1. In order to be processed by the College, a complaint must be filed in writing to the Ethics Committee of the College within three years of the date of discovery of the alleged violation; and the Committee has the responsibility to look into incidents brought to its attention regardless of the informality of the information, provided the information can be documented or supported or may be a matter of public record. The three-year period within which a complaint must be filed shall temporarily cease to run during intervals when the accused member is in inactive status, or when the accused member resigns from the College.

2. The Committee chairman initially will determine whether the complaint falls within the purview of the Ethics Committee and whether immediate investigation is necessary. However, all letters of complaint that are filed with the Ethics Committee will appear on the agenda of the next committee meeting. The Ethics Committee shall have the final discretion to determine whether a complaint falls within the purview of the Ethics Committee.

Reprinted with permission of the American College of Healthcare Executives.

3. If a grievance proceeding is initiated by the Ethics Committee:
    a. Specifics of the complaint will be sent to the respondent by
        certified mail. In such mailing, committee staff will inform the
        respondent that the grievance proceeding has been initiated, and
        that the respondent may respond directly to the Ethics Committee;
        the respondent also will be asked to cooperate with the Regent
        investigating the complaint.
    b. The Ethics Committee shall refer the matter to the appropriate
        Regent who is deemed best able to investigate the alleged infrac-
        tion. The Regent shall make inquiry into the matter, and in the
        process the respondent shall be given an opportunity to be heard.
    c. Upon completion of the inquiry, the Regent shall present a com-
        plete report and recommended disposition of the matter in writing
        to the Ethics Committee. Absent unusual circumstances, the Re-
        gent is expected to complete his or her report and recommended
        disposition and provide them to the Committee within 60 days.
4. Upon the Committee's receipt of the Regent's report and recommended
    disposition, the Committee shall review them and make its written
    recommendation to the Board of Governors as to what action shall be
    taken and the reason or reasons therefor. A copy of the Committee's
    recommended decision along with the Regent's report and recommended
    disposition to the Board will be mailed to the respondent by certified mail.
    In such mailing, the respondent will be notified that within 30 days after
    his or her receipt of the Ethics Committee's recommended decision, the
    respondent may file a written appeal of the recommended decision with
    the Board of Governors.
5. Any written appeal submitted by the respondent must be received by the
    Board of Governors within 30 days after the recommended decision of the
    Ethics Committee is received by the respondent. The Board of Governors
    shall not take action on the Ethics Committee's recommended decision
    until the 30-day appeal period has elapsed. If no appeal to the Board of
    Governors is filed in a timely fashion, the Board shall review the recom-
    mended decision and determine action to be taken.
6. If an appeal to the Board of Governors is timely filed, the College
    Chairman shall appoint an ad hoc committee consisting of three Fellows
    to hear the matter. At least 30 days' notice of the formation of this commit-
    tee, and of the hearing date, time, and place, with an opportunity for
    representation, shall be mailed to the respondent. Reasonable requests for
    postponement shall be given consideration.
7. This ad hoc committee shall give the respondent adequate opportunity to
    present his or her case at the hearing, including the opportunity to submit
    a written statement and other documents deemed relevant by the respon-

dent, and to be represented if so desired. Within a reasonable period of time following the hearing, the ad hoc committee shall write a detailed report with recommendations to the Board of Governors.

8. The Board of Governors shall decide what action to take after reviewing the report of the ad hoc committee. The Board shall provide the respondent with a copy of its decision. The decision of the Board of Governors shall be final. The Board of Governors shall have the authority to accept or reject any of the findings or recommended decisions of the Regent, the Ethics Committee, or the ad hoc committee, and to order whatever level of discipline it feels is justified.

9. At each level of the grievance proceeding, the Board of Governors shall have the sole discretion to notify or contact the complainant relating to the grievance proceeding; provided, however, that the complainant shall be notified as to whether the complaint was reviewed by the Ethics Committee and whether the Ethics Committee or the Board of Governors has taken final action with respect to the complaint.

10. No individual shall serve on the ad hoc committee described above, or otherwise participate in these grievance proceedings on behalf of the College, if he or she is in direct economic competition with the respondent or otherwise has a financial conflict of interest in the matter, unless such conflict is disclosed to and waived in writing by the respondent.

11. All information obtained, reviewed, discussed, and otherwise used or developed in a grievance proceeding that is not otherwise publicly known, publicly available, or part of the public domain is considered to be privileged and strictly confidential information of the College, and is not to be disclosed to anyone outside of the grievance proceeding except as determined by the Board of Governors or as required by law; provided, however, that an individual's membership status is not confidential and may be made available to the public upon request.

APPENDIX II

Ethics Committee Action

Once the grievance proceeding has been initiated, the Ethics Committee may take any of the following actions based upon its findings:

1. Determine the grievance complaint to be invalid.
2. Dismiss the grievance complaint.
3. Recommend censure.
4. Recommend transfer to inactive status for a specified minimum period of time.
5. Recommend expulsion.

Reprinted with permission of the American College of Healthcare Executives.

References

1. Moore, J. 1996. "The Pharmaceutical Industry." *National Health Policy Forum* January: 2.
2. Burns, L. R. 1997. "Physician Practice Management Companies." *Health Care Management Review* 22 (4): 32.
3. Kertesz, L. 1997. "Quiet Giant." *Modern Healthcare* March 10: 91–93.
4. Kaiser-Permanente. 1996. Annual Report. San Francisco.
5. Manor Care Inc. 1996. Annual Report. Gaithersburg, MD.
6. Longest, B. 1980. *Management Practice for the Health Professional*. Reston, VA: Reston, 45–50.
7. Mintzberg, H. 1973. *The Nature of Managerial Work*. New York: Harper & Row.
8. Quinn, R. E., S. R. Faerman, M. P. Thompson, and M. R. McGrath. 1996. *Becoming a Master Manager: A Competency Framework*, 2nd ed. New York: Wiley & Sons, 1–28.
9. Allison, R. F., W. L. Dowling, and F. C. Munson. 1975. "The Role of the Health Services Administrator and Implications for Education." In *Education for Health Administration*, vol. 2. Chicago: Health Administration Press, 147–84.
10. Kovner, A. R. 1984. *Really Trying: A Career Guide for the Health Services Manager*. Chicago: Health Administration Press, 194–203.
11. Brown, R. 1966. *Judgment in Administration*. New York: McGraw-Hill, 14–21.
12. Goleman, D. 1998. "What Makes a Leader." *Harvard Business Review* Nov–Dec: 93–102.
13. Boyatzis, R. E. 1995. "Cornerstones of Change: Building the Path for Self-Directed Learning." In *Innovation in Professional Education* by R. E. Boyatzis, S. Cowan, D. Kolb, and associates. San Francisco: Jossey-Bass, 50–59.
14. Perrow, C. 1982. "Disintegrating Social Sciences." *Phi Delta Kappan* 63: 684–88.
15. Goleman, D. 1998. "What Makes a Leader?" *Harvard Business Review* Nov-Dec: 92–105.

16. Kovner, A. R. 1988. *Really Managing: The Work of Effective CEOs in Large Health Organizations.* Chicago: Health Administration Press, 129–54.
17. Rindler, M. 1992. *The Challenge of Hospital Governance.* Chicago: American Hospital Publishing, 169–71.
18. Grove, A. S. 1985. *High Output Management.* New York: Vintage Press.
19. Walton, M. 1980. *The Deming Management Method.* New York: Putnam.
20. "Performance Payback." 1996. *Modern Healthcare.* July 13: 39–46.
21. Victory, J. O. 1999. Personal communication.
22. Burgess, J. 1992. Personal communication.
23. Webber, R. A. 1972. *Time and Management.* New York: Van Nostrand Rheinhold.
24. Block, P. 1987. *The Empowered Manager.* San Francisco: Jossey-Bass, 137–60.
25. Walton, M. *Op. cit.*
26. Griffith, J. R. 1999. *The Well-Managed Healthcare Organization*, 4th ed. Chicago: Health Administration Press.
27. Freidson, E. 1972. *Profession of Medicine.* New York: Dodd, Mead.
28. Lindblom, C. F. 1977. *Politics and Markets.* New York: Basic Books.
29. Saltman, A. B., and D. W. Young. 1981. "The Hospital Power Equilibrium: An Alternative View of the Cost Containment Dilemma." *Journal of Health Politics, Policy & Law* 6: 408–10.
30. Joint Commission on Accreditation of Healthcare Organizations. 1998. *Accreditation Manual for Hospitals.* Oakbrook Terrace, IL: Joint Commission.
31. Slater, C. 1980. "The Physician Manager's Role: Results of a Survey." In *The Physician in Management*, edited by R. Schenke. Washington, D.C.: American Academy of Medical Directors, 57–69.
32. Peters, T. 1987. *Thriving on Chaos: Handbook for a Managerial Revolution.* New York: Alfred A. Knopf.
33. Weick, K. 1979. *The Social Psychology of Organizing*, 2nd ed. Reading, MA: Addison-Wesley.
34. Kalbhen, J. 1999. "Search Engine." *Hospitals & Health Networks* 73 (1): 16.
35. Tyler, J. L. 1998. *Tyler's Guide: The Healthcare Executive's Job Search*, 2nd ed. Chicago: Health Administration Press, 85–87.
36. Wells, S. J. 1999. "Site-Seeing: Health-Care Information." *The New York Times,* January 7.

Suggestions for Future Reading

A BASIC SET OF MANAGEMENT BOOKS FOR HEALTHCARE EXECUTIVES

Bryson, J. R. 1995. *Strategic Planning for Public and Nonprofit Organization*, rev. ed. San Francisco: Jossey-Bass.

Block, P. 1987. *The Empowered Manager*. San Francisco: Jossey-Bass.

Griffith, J. R. 1993. *The Moral Challenges of Health Care Management*. Chicago: Health Administration Press.

Griffith, J. R. 1995. *The Well-Managed Health Care Organization*, 3rd ed. Chicago: Health Administration Press.

Griffith, J. R., V. K. Sahney, and R. A. Mohr. 1995. *Reengineering Health Care*. Chicago: Health Administration Press.

Herzlinger, R. E. 1997. *Market-Driven Health Care*. Reading, MA: Addison-Wesley.

Maister, D. H. 1993. *Managing the Professional Service Firm*. New York: Free Press.

O'Toole, J. 1995. *Leading Change*. San Francisco: Jossey-Bass.

Peters, T. 1987. *Thriving on Chaos: Handbook for a Managerial Revolution*. New York: Knopf.

Volesko, M. M. 1998. *The RWJF Internet Handbook: Basic Specialized, Health Care and Grant-Seeking Resources on the World Wide Web*. Princeton, NJ: Robert Wood Johnson Foundation.

A BASIC SET OF MANAGEMENT JOURNALS FOR HEALTHCARE EXECUTIVES

Frontiers of Health Services Management, Foundation of the American College of Healthcare Executives, One North Franklin Street, Suite 1700, Chicago, IL 60606-3491.

Harvard Business Review, 60 Harvard Way, Boston, MA 02163.

Health Affairs, Project HOPE, Suite 600, 7500 Old Georgetown Road, Bethesda, MD 20814.

Journal of Healthcare Management, Foundation of the American College of Healthcare Executives, One North Franklin Street, Suite 1700, Chicago, IL 60606-3491.

Modern Healthcare, 740 N. Rush St., Chicago, IL 60611-2590.

For a more comprehensive annotated bibliography of books, articles, and journals relevant to healthcare management, see Kovner, A. R., and D. Neuhauser. 1997. *Health Services Management: Readings and Commentary*, 6th ed. Chicago: Health Administration Press, 519–522.

Index

About the Authors

ANTHONY R. KOVNER, PH.D., IS A PROFESSOR of management at the Robert F. Wagner Graduate School of Public Service at New York University. He has served as director of the Hospital Community Benefit Standards Program (HCBSP), a W. K. Kellogg program to encourage the implementation of systematic community benefit services programs for hospitals. He is a member of the board of trustees for Lutheran Medical Center. Before joining New York University, Dr. Kovner was chief executive officer of the Newcomb Hospital of Vineland, New Jersey, and senior health consultant of the United Auto Workers union in Detroit, Michigan. Dr. Kovner is the author of *Really Managing: The Work of Effective CEOs in Large Health Organizations* as well as numerous books and articles about health services management. He received the 1999 Filerman Prize for Educational Leadership, awarded by the Association of University Programs in Health Administration (AUPHA).

ALAN H. CHANNING, M.S., FACHE, IS THE PRESIDENT and chief executive officer of St. Vincent Charity Hospital and Saint Luke's Medical Center in Cleveland, Ohio. He is a clinical assistant professor at the Ohio State University Graduate Program in Health Services Management and Policy. He has served as Visiting Healthcare Executive at the New York University Wagner Graduate School of Public Service. He has been the executive director of several major public hospitals, including Bellevue Hospital Center in New York City. He has served in senior management roles at university hospitals, community hospitals, and an HMO. Mr. Channing is a consultant to the Joint Commission on Accreditation of Healthcare Organizations and the Commission on Accreditation of Rehabilitation Facilities. He is a Fellow of the American College of Healthcare Executives. In addition, he serves as a lecturer for several universities.